TOP 101 INVENTIONS OF ALL TIME!

Intriguing Facts and Trivia About History's Greatest Inventions!

SCOTT MATTHEWS

Copyright © 2023 Scott Matthews

All rights reserved. No part of this publication may be reproduced, distributed or transmitted in any form or by any means, including photocopying, recording, or other electronic or mechanical methods, without the prior written permission of the publisher, except in the case of brief quotations embodied in critical reviews and certain other non-commercial uses permitted by copyright law.

Trademarked names appear throughout this book. Rather than use a trademark symbol with every occurrence of a trademarked name, names are used in an editorial fashion, with no intention of infringement of the respective owner's trademark. The information in this book is distributed on an "as is" basis, without warranty. Although every precaution has been taken in the preparation of this work, neither the author nor the publisher shall have any liability to any person or entity with respect to any loss or damage caused or alleged to be caused directly or indirectly by the information contained in this book.

The more that you read, the more things you will know. The more you learn, the more places you'll go. - Dr. Seuss

Contents

Introduction	vii
1. Wheel	1
2. Printing press	2
3. Lightbulb	3
4. Telephone	4
5. Steam engine	5
6. Airplane	6
7. Automobile	8
8. Coffee maker	9
9. Camera	10
10. Phonograph	11
11. Telegraph	12
12. Computer	13
13. Internet	14
14. Penicillin	15
15. Books	16
16. Fire	17
17. Nails	18
18. Optical lenses	19
19. Paper currency	20
20. Gunpowder	22
21. Electricity	24
22. Steel	25
23. Antibiotics	26
24. Paper	28
25. Vaccine	29
26. Floppy disk	30
27. Toaster	32
28. Electron microscope	33
29. MRI machine	34
30. Prednisone	35
31. Cell phone	36
32. X-ray machine	38
33. Nitroglycerin	39

34. Bluetooth	40
35. DNA fingerprinting	41
36. Wi-Fi	43
37. Hypodermic syringe	44
38. GPS	46
39. USB drive	47
40. Thermometer	48
41. Copernican Theory	50
42. Central heating	51
43. Gregorian calendar	52
44. Pacemaker	54
45. Online streaming	55
46. Manufactured insulin	56
47. Internal combustion engine	57
48. Cochlear prosthetics	58
49. Morphine	59
50. Dissolvable sutures	60
51. Laser	61
52. Microwave oven	62
53. Clock	63
54. Concrete	65
55. Compact disc	66
56. Fire extinguisher	67
57. Cleats	68
58. Washing machine	69
59. Dishwasher	70
60. CT machine	72
61. DNA sequencers	74
62. Porcelain veneers	75
63. Albuterol sulfate	76
64. Flush toilet	78
65. Cardiac defibrillators	79
66. Soap	80
67. Moving assembly line	81
68. Telescope	82
69. Radio	83
70. Cloud storage systems	84
71. Dialysis machine	85
72. Public trash disposal	86
73. Toothpaste	87
74. Public libraries	88

75. Fertilizer	90
76. EMDR Therapy	92
77. Pasteurization	93
78. Barometer	94
79. Microscope	96
80. Compression socks	97
81. Atomic bomb	100
82. Text messaging	102
83. Heart-lung machine	103
84. Non-steroidal anti-inflammatory drugs	104
85. Television	105
86. Petrol	106
87. Beta-blockers	107
88. VHS	108
89. Public transportation	109
90. Theory of evolution	111
91. Carbon dating	113
92. Hindu Arabic numeral system	114
93. Smartphone	115
94. DVD	116
95. Refrigerator	118
96. Dentures	119
97. Prozac	120
98. Electric motor	122
99. Dental braces	123
100. Air conditioner	124
101. Calculus	127
102. References	128

Introduction

Since the dawn of humanity, our evolutionary journey has been marked not just by physical adaptations but by a relentless drive to innovate. When faced with challenges, we didn't just adapt—we invented. From the rudimentary stone tools wielded by our earliest ancestors to the dazzling digital technologies of today, our history as a species is indelibly intertwined with our history as inventors.

The story of human invention is a testament to our boundless imagination, our capacity to envision a better future, and our tenacity to transform those visions into reality. It's a narrative that spans every culture, era, and corner of the globe. Whether grand or humble, each invention has its unique tale of necessity, serendipity, and human spirit.

So, as you turn the pages of this tome, be prepared to marvel at the heights of human achievement. In celebrating the top inventions, we celebrate the best of what it means to be human: our drive, passion, and an unyielding desire to push the boundaries of what's possible.

Although I've made every effort to encompass the breadth of significant inventions—sourced from myriad lists and focused on recurring mentions—the arrangement is arbitrary. So, immerse yourself in this captivating realm of creativity and innovation. Welcome to the exhilarating voyage of human brilliance. Let's embark!

1. Wheel

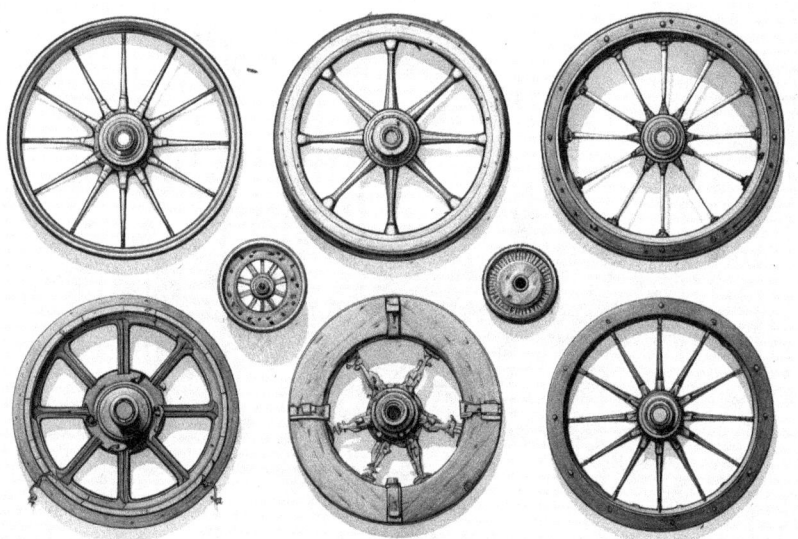

The wheel is one of the most transformative advancements in human history. Originating around 3500 BC in the ancient lands of Mesopotamia, its primary purpose was surprisingly humble: aiding in pottery-making. Yet, as its potential was recognized, the wheel transitioned from crafting clay to becoming a driving force behind transportation, especially when incorporated into chariots. This evolution revolutionized our entire concept of movement, laying the groundwork for modern transportation systems. Early societies benefited from the wheel's efficiency, making long-distance trade smoother and paving the way for richer cultural exchanges and idea-sharing. Furthermore, the advent of the wheel marked a significant shift in construction techniques, simplifying the task of relocating heavy materials and leading to more ambitious architectural feats.

2. Printing press

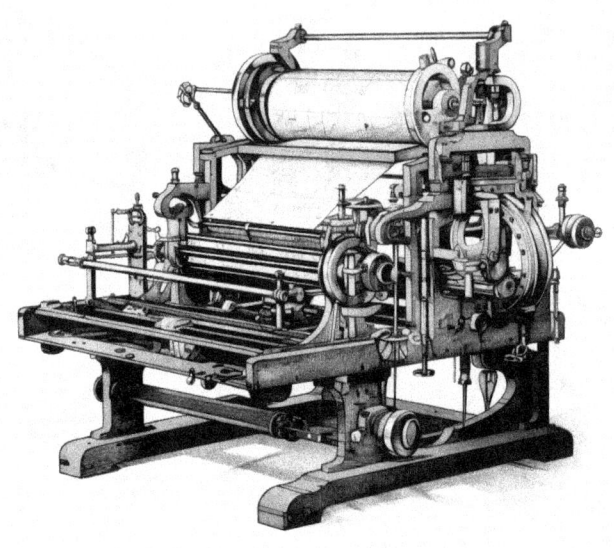

In the mid-15th century, Johannes Gutenberg changed the world with his invention of the printing press. Before this, making books was a long, tedious task done by hand. Gutenberg's press turned things around, allowing for quick, cheaper production of many copies. This change wasn't about faster printing; it revolutionized how knowledge spread. More people could now own books, giving everyone a chance to learn and read. The press also made it easier to print other things, like pamphlets, which were crucial in spreading new ideas during the Enlightenment and Protestant Reformation. Today, this groundbreaking invention paved the way for modern printing techniques, and its influence remains strong in how we share and access information.

3. Lightbulb

The lightbulb, an iconic invention, changed how we light up our homes and workplaces, hugely improving our productivity and daily lives. Before this, people relied on expensive, less efficient candles and oil lamps. Then, the lightbulb came along, offering a better, cost-effective way to brighten spaces. While there were some early attempts at creating electric lighting, the real breakthrough came in 1879 with Thomas Edison's design. He smartly used a vacuum-sealed bulb with a carbon filament, preventing it from burning too quickly. This genius invention quickly spread, changing how we lived and worked. And even today, lightbulbs continue to evolve, becoming more energy-efficient and versatile in their uses.

4. Telephone

The telephone is a game-changer in communication, redefining business and personal connections. Before it came around, people mainly depended on face-to-face chats or written letters, which had their drawbacks in terms of speed. But in 1876, Alexander Graham Bell introduced the telephone, despite similar work by others. His model transformed voice into electrical signals using a transmitter and receiver connected by a wire. This invention quickly became popular, making communication faster and easier. Today, the telephone's legacy continues to thrive. From old landlines to the latest smartphones, the phone's evolution ensures we stay connected effortlessly, emphasizing its lasting importance in our lives.

5. Steam engine

The steam engine, a groundbreaking invention, was crucial in driving the Industrial Revolution and shaping modern industries. This engine, which works by turning water into steam to move pistons or turbines, was introduced by James Watt in the early 18th century. First used to help with mine pumps, it soon became crucial for powering steam trains and boats. By using steam, an easy-to-get and affordable fuel, machines could work faster, boosting productivity. This change had a massive effect on society, kickstarting the Industrial Revolution in the late 18th century. It brought about the era of big factories and faster transport, making moving goods and people around simpler. Today, while other power sources have taken over in many areas, the steam engine's influence remains undeniable.

6. Airplane

Airplanes, majestic marvels of human innovation, have revolutionized our understanding of time and space. Born from the audacious dreams of pioneers like the Wright brothers, who took to the skies in the early 20th century, these machines transformed the canvas of global connectivity. No longer did vast oceans and expansive lands dictate the limitations of human interaction. Their significance transcends mere transportation. On the civilian front, airplanes ushered in a new era of global tourism, shrinking our vast world into reachable destinations. Long-distance relationships, both personal and professional, now thrived with newfound vigor. The skies buzzed with stories of reunions, explorations, and dreams realized. In the realms of commerce and trade, the airplane rendered borders porous, accelerating the global economy. Essential goods, from life-saving medicines to exotic fruits, could now reach corners of the world previously deemed too remote. And yet, their might isn't just consigned to peaceful endeavors. Airplanes have played pivotal roles in shaping the outcomes of wars and diplomatic interventions. Their versatility has been tested time and again, from reconnaissance missions to humanitarian aid drops. Technological advancements have refined these aerial juggernauts over time. Powerful jet engines, coupled with advanced materials like aluminum and composite plastics, have enhanced their endurance, efficiency, and safety. But perhaps the airplane's most profound impact lies in its cultural contributions. It has bridged cultures, fostered understanding, and seeded shared experiences.

7. Automobile

Karl Benz, the visionary German engineer, etched his name in automotive history between 1885-1886, crafting the Benz Patent-Motorwagen. This gasoline-powered innovation, bearing semblance to a three-wheeled carriage, was equipped with a singular cylinder and a four-stroke engine. While its humble pace of ten miles per hour and a twenty-five-mile range might seem modest by today's standards, it heralded a bold leap in vehicular evolution. But the saga didn't stop there. The mantle was soon taken up by luminaries like Henry Ford, whose 1908 brainchild, the iconic Model T, transformed the automobile landscape. Marrying ingenuity with industrial prowess, Ford democratized the car, making it an affordable, everyday marvel. Today, the resonance of their innovations is palpable, with cars weaving tales of human endeavors and aspirations on roads that stretch across every continent.

8. Coffee maker

Coffee has been a popular drink since long before the existence of the coffee maker. Beans were first ground, then steeped in boiling water, with a particular section of the pot capturing residual grinds. However, as times changed, so did brewing methods. The shift led to drip coffee, where boiling water percolated through coffee grounds contained by a porous material - sometimes even cloth or socks! In 1908, Melitta Bentz revolutionized this with her invention: a machine that used blotting paper to filter grinds, setting the stage for modern drip brewing. Since then, coffee machines have evolved, focusing on user-friendly designs and speedy brewing, ensuring that the morning cup remains a cherished ritual.

9. Camera

The world of photography owes its inception to pioneers like Charles and Vincent Chevalier, who crafted the first wooden camera, and Joseph Nicephore Niepce, who marked history by capturing the first still image with it. Early photographic endeavors harnessed silver iodide and mercury vapor, requiring hours of light exposure. But innovation was relentless. From hours, the wait time dwindled to thirty minutes, then minutes, and eventually, the magic of capturing moments became instantaneous. Though initially a domain for elite photographers, by 1888, households began acquiring cameras, igniting a photography trend. This shift fostered businesses dedicated to developing photographs. However, as the adage goes, change is the only constant. The digital camera's advent sidelined traditional development, empowering people to immortalize and print moments at their leisure.

10. Phonograph

Before 1877, music's joy was ephemeral, alive only in the fleeting moments it was performed. Then, Thomas Edison changed everything with his invention of the phonograph. Initially, it relied on cylinders to produce melodies, which were soon succeeded by disks. The device's magic lay in a needle tracing grooves on these disks, translating them into musical vibrations. Paired with a flaring horn, these delicate sounds were magnified, allowing households to relish music without live performers — a concept once unthinkable. Some models even integrated rudimentary headphones, mirroring stethoscopes in design, for a more intimate listening experience. While the march of time ushered in diverse music formats, overshadowing phonographs and vinyl, these vintage treasures still enchant enthusiasts, offering a tactile connection to music's rich past.

11. Telegraph

Before the telegraph's advent, messages traveled at the speed of a horse, carried by letters that took days or even months to reach their recipients, making timely communication challenging. Enter the telegraph, a revolutionary invention. Though Francis Ronalds crafted an early version in 1816 using static electricity, the Cooke and Wheatstone system, initially serving the locomotive sector, gained widespread acclaim. The telegraph transformed the pace of communication. Initially, messages zipped along wires in the dots and dashes of Morse code, but over time, systems evolved to send messages in plain English. While today's world has moved beyond the telegraph, its legacy is undeniable, laying the groundwork for modern communication and forever changing the tempo of human interaction.

12. Computer

Computers, once mammoth and exclusive to elite tasks, have evolved into ubiquitous tools, reshaping vast swathes of modern life from communication to commerce. Born in the mid-20th century, early computers, limited by size and cost, were champions of scientific and military pursuits. Yet, waves of technological progress, including advances in materials, software, and processing power, have transformed them into compact powerhouses. Today's computers, versatile and accessible, permeate industries from business and medicine to entertainment and education. Serving as the backbone of contemporary society, they efficiently process vast data, bridging gaps in communication and revolutionizing work and leisure.

13. Internet

The Internet, originating as a military research project in the 1960s, has grown into a colossal web of interconnected networks, enabling seamless global communication and reshaping countless aspects of modern life, from business to social interactions. Born from the US Department of Defense's ARPANET initiative, it aimed to boost communication among scattered researchers. Today, it links billions worldwide, driven by continuous technological innovations in hardware and software and the development of advanced communication protocols. This digital nexus has not only transformed how we communicate, learn, and entertain ourselves but has also crafted new economic and social realms, cementing its central role in today's interconnected world.

14. Penicillin

Penicillin is a famous antibiotic that changed the medical world by effectively treating many bacterial infections. Its discovery occurred in 1928 when Alexander Fleming noticed that the mold, Penicillium notatum, had special properties that could fight bacteria. This big find earned him the Nobel Prize in Medicine in 1945, marking it as a turning point in healthcare. Thanks to penicillin, many illnesses like pneumonia, strep throat, and certain skin and urinary infections, which used to be very dangerous, became much easier to treat. This discovery saved countless lives and started a new chapter in medicine, making many infectious diseases less deadly. Now, because of penicillin and other antibiotics that followed, we have much better chances against many bacterial infections.

15. Books

From scrolls to screens, the evolution of books mirrors humanity's quest to preserve knowledge. Around 4000 BC, the ancient world turned to papyrus scrolls, using paper derived from a similarly named plant. While these scrolls held information, their elongated form made reading a task. Around 100 BC, the Romans introduced the codex – a precursor to the modern book. Bound in wood and transcribed by dedicated scribes, codices revolutionized reading. They were portable, making religious texts handier, and could lay flat on a table, a boon for scholars and note-takers. Fast forward to today: while the essence remains unchanged, the medium has shifted from hand-written pages to mass-printed volumes and even digital eBooks, making knowledge more accessible than ever.

16. Fire

The story of fire's beginnings is wrapped in a mystery, reaching far back into the early moments of humankind, long before we started writing history. While we can't pinpoint the exact moment of discovery, there are plenty of theories. Some believe early humans first saw fire after natural events, like lightning touching dry grass. These chance encounters might have taught them how to use and control fire. Another idea is that our ancestors discovered fire by trying things themselves, figuring out that rubbing sticks together or hitting rocks could produce sparks, leading to a flame. Once they understood fire, its benefits became clear: warmth, cooking food, and safety from wild animals. Fire played a considerable role in our growth as a civilization, helping us make tools, grow food, and build more prominent communities. Even today, we rely on fire in many ways, from energy to cooking, but we also recognize its dangers if not handled with care.

17. Nails

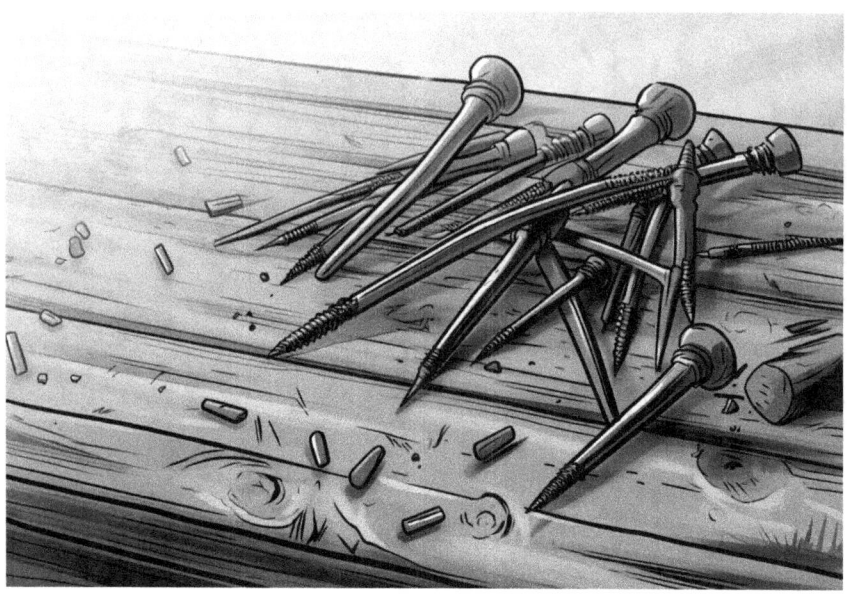

Nails, with their vast types and uses, have a long-standing history dating back to ancient civilizations. Though the exact origins of the first nail remain somewhat mysterious, we've found early versions made from metals like bronze and iron, which were used not just for function but also as decorative pieces. The Middle Ages saw a notable improvement in nail craftsmanship. Blacksmiths, masters of metalwork, developed refined techniques, catering to the needs of growing architectural wonders and societal demands. As time progressed, advances in metal sciences and machinery revolutionized nail production, leading to the varied and precise nails we see today, made from materials like steel, aluminum, and copper. Their widespread use in construction and crafts highlights their significant role in shaping human history.

18. Optical lenses

Dating back to antiquity, optical lenses have been integral to human innovation, with ancient civilizations like the Egyptians, Greeks, and Romans employing polished crystals or glass for varied purposes. The transformative leap to the sophisticated optical lens of today primarily emerged in the 17th century, credited mainly to the Dutch polymath Antonie van Leeuwenhoek. Recognized as a luminary in microscopy, van Leeuwenhoek's pioneering creations birthed the high-powered microscope, revealing the fascinating world of microorganisms to human eyes. His lens, distinctively spherical and meticulously hand-crafted, surpassed the magnification and clarity of traditional convex lenses. Van Leeuwenhoek's ingenuity didn't stop there; he also refined lens-making processes, ensuring superior precision and image resolution. Fast-forward to today, and optical lenses permeate various facets of life, from corrective eyewear and cameras to advanced telescopes and microscopes, underscoring their continued significance in scientific and everyday spheres.

19. Paper currency

Paper currency, widely recognized as banknotes, traces its origins to the historic corridors of ancient China during the Tang Dynasty (618-907 AD). First emerging in the 7th century, these initial incarnations of paper money found favor among merchants and traders, offering a practical substitute for the cumbersome metal coinage of the era. As its practicality became apparent, the concept of paper money transcended the boundaries of Asia, eventually making its mark in Europe during the 17th century, with Sweden leading the charge. Subsequent adopters included nations such as England and the United States. At the heart of paper currency's advent was a quest for a more streamlined, lightweight means of exchange that simultaneously provided enhanced security against counterfeiting. This was achieved by crafting banknotes with intricate designs and protective features. In the contemporary financial landscape, paper currency holds steadfast, symbolizing trust and facilitating transactions in countless economies worldwide. However, in the face of technological advances and the rise of digital currencies like Bitcoin, the once-uncontested dominion of paper currency stands at a crossroads. The upcoming chapters of financial history may witness a subtle shift as digital transactions eclipse the tangible legacy of banknotes.

20. Gunpowder

Gunpowder originated in ancient China and was a groundbreaking invention developed around the 9th century. It's thought that it was accidentally discovered by alchemists searching for a magical life-extending elixir. Initially used for entertainment and celebrations, it didn't take long for its military uses to be recognized. Using gunpowder, the Chinese developed powerful tools like bombs, rockets, and other weapons. This revolutionary substance spread from China throughout Asia and later to Europe, changing how wars were fought. With the advent of gunpowder, battles like the Mongol conquests, the Hundred Years' War, and the Napoleonic Wars were influenced. Today, gunpowder is still found in various firearms, even with the advent of newer propellants. Its role in reshaping global warfare and technological advancements remains unmatched.

Did You Know?

The term "Uncanny Valley" is a concept in robotics and artificial intelligence where human-like robots or characters cause a sense of unease or discomfort as they become almost, but not quite, identical to real humans. The closer they get to looking human, without being perfectly human-like, the more unsettling they become.

Dive into some fascinating facets of this psychological phenomenon:

• Origins: The term was first coined by the Japanese roboticist Masahiro Mori in 1970. He noticed that as robots became more human-like, people would have a more emotional and positive response, but only up to a point. Beyond this point, the response would suddenly turn strongly negative before becoming positive again once the appearance was indistinguishably human.

• Movies and Animation: CGI characters and animated figures in movies sometimes fall into the Uncanny Valley, leading audiences to feel discomfort. An example is the animated film "The Polar Express," where some viewers found the characters' expressions eerie.

• Real-Life Applications: As humanoid robots become more prevalent in industries like healthcare and service, understanding the Uncanny Valley is vital to ensure people can interact comfortably with these machines.

• Psychological Roots: Some psychologists believe the Uncanny Valley taps into our primal fear of death or lifelessness. Others suggest it might be rooted in an evolutionary aversion to beings that look human but move differently, signaling illness or a threat.

As technology advances, understanding our emotional responses becomes as crucial as the tech itself.

21. Electricity

The tale of electricity is not the brainchild of one solitary genius but the cumulative legacy of countless thinkers, experimenters, and innovators. The ancient Greeks were among the first to flirt with its potential, noting the mysterious static sparks. This curiosity persisted, lighting the imaginative fires of many throughout the Middle Ages and the Renaissance. Fast forward to the 18th century: enter Benjamin Franklin with his audacious kite experiment in a storm, famously bridging the link between lightning and electricity. The 19th century then witnessed a rapid electrical evolution. Alessandro Volta birthed the idea of the battery, and Michael Faraday unraveled the wonders of electromagnetic induction and sketched the very essence of electric fields. At the same time, Thomas Edison illuminated our world with the incandescent bulb and drafted the blueprint for the first-ever electric power network. Today, electricity isn't just a scientific wonder—it's the lifeblood of our modern world, lighting up homes, driving industries, and inspiring future innovations.

22. Steel

The journey of steel production reaches back to ancient civilizations, but the modern method owes a significant debt to the 19th century. It was Sir Henry Bessemer, a British visionary, who stood out for devising a transformative mass-production approach. His revolutionary Bessemer process involved a simple but effective technique: by introducing air into molten iron, impurities, and surplus carbon were removed, leading to the birth of a more robust and durable form of iron. This ingenious method changed the landscape of the steel industry, making quality steel more affordable and accessible on an unmatched scale. While technological advances have introduced newer techniques like the open-hearth furnace and the basic oxygen process, Bessemer's contribution remains a pivotal chapter in steel production's history. Today, steel is an omnipresent force, integral to various sectors, from towering skyscrapers and zipping vehicles to the multitude of products shaping our everyday existence.

23. Antibiotics

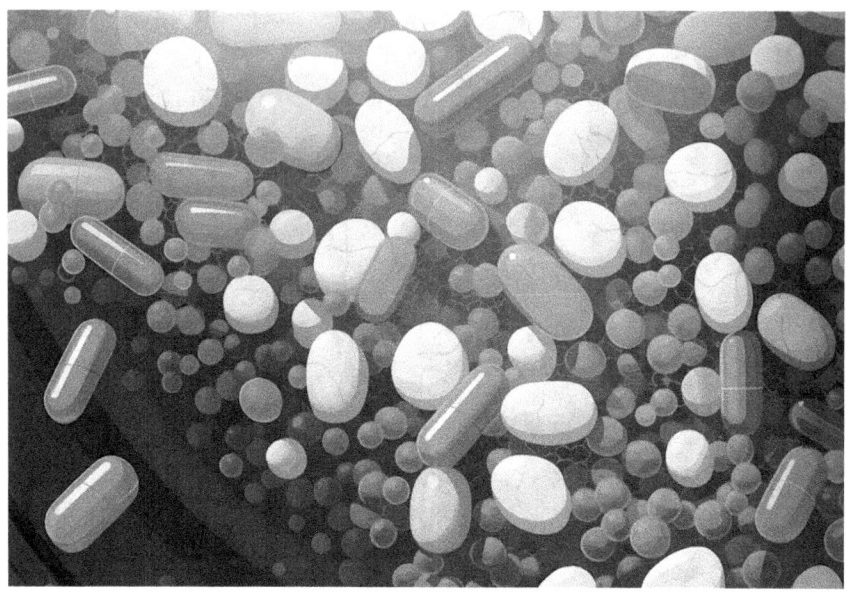

In 1928, a forgotten petri dish in Alexander Fleming's lab became the birthplace of a medical revolution. This Scottish microbiologist noticed something peculiar: a mold, known as Penicillium notatum, was preventing the growth of surrounding bacteria. This mold's secret? A substance that would soon become the world's first antibiotic—penicillin. While Fleming pioneered recognizing penicillin's potential, it took a collaborative effort spearheaded by Howard Florey and Ernst Chain to bring its healing properties to the masses. As World War II raged, they championed the large-scale production of penicillin and proved its might in clinical trials, showcasing its unparalleled prowess against bacterial infections. The introduction of antibiotics marked a seismic shift in medicine. Suddenly, once-deadly, infections were treatable, and countless lives were salvaged. Today, antibiotics remain essential tools in the medical toolkit. However, our heavy reliance on them has cast a shadow: the rise of antibiotic-resistant bacteria. This emerging challenge underscores the need for prudence and innovation in deploying these life-saving drugs.

24. Paper

Paper's journey began in ancient China, with early crafters transforming tree bark and plant fibers into rudimentary sheets as far back as the 2nd century BC. This primitive process involved mashing plant fibers into a pulp and laying them out to dry. Over time, the Chinese fine-tuned their methods, adopting water-powered mills and integrating resilient fibers like bamboo and mulberry bark. This craft, once a regional secret, soon found its way to places like the Islamic territories and Europe, where it saw further enhancements. Today, despite our digital age, paper remains ubiquitous, vital for tasks from writing and printing to packaging. And as its global demand persists, the spotlight shines on sustainable paper-making techniques to reduce environmental impact.

25. Vaccine

Vaccines are special substances that train our immune system to fight off certain diseases. They play a huge role in public health, helping stop the spread of illnesses and reducing the number of people who get seriously sick or die from them. The idea of vaccination started in the 18th century, with the smallpox vaccine being a significant breakthrough. This vaccine was a game-changer because it helped eliminate a dangerous and highly contagious disease. Since then, we've made vaccines for many other diseases, including measles, polio, flu, and hepatitis. These shots have had a significant impact, saving countless lives by preventing or even getting rid of some diseases. This success comes from understanding our immune system better and knowing more about the germs causing diseases. Today, vaccines are a crucial part of global health efforts, constantly used to protect us from the spread of infections.

26. Floppy disk

Today, the floppy disk is a relic of the past, with the most common reminder of its existence being the "save" symbol on most word processing applications. However, when floppy disks were first invented, they greatly benefited society. These disks were enclosed in a plastic covering, protecting them from accidental scratches. They acted as digital storage devices and were created by IBM in the 1960s. They were not commercially available until the 1970s, however. Soon, a battle broke out to produce floppy disks that could hold more data while taking up less physical space. The original disks were eight inches in diameter, but over time advancements led to the creation of disks as compact as just one inch in diameter. In the 1990s, however, the size of popular programs began to make floppy disks seem impractical, as dozens of disks were sometimes required to install a single application. This led to their eventual replacement by CD-ROMs. However, from 1960-1990, the floppy disk was the sole device allowing an easy transfer of data, allowing for the development of computer history as we know it.

27. Toaster

In the modern world, toast is considered one of the easiest options when making breakfast. You can pop a few pieces of bread inside of a toaster, wait a few moments, and then collect your perfectly made toast. However, making toast was not always a simple process. Before the invention of the toaster, people would have to toast pieces of bread over a fire with only a metal fork to hold it in place. This process was time-consuming and often led to burnt pieces of toast. The first toaster was officially made in 1909 by Frank Shailor and was called the D-12 model. It became popular quickly and led to further inventions such as Copeman Electric Stove Company's "toaster that turns toast," which allowed a person to make toast without rotating it by hand. Soon, in 1921, Charles Strite created the pop-up toaster we commonly find in most kitchens. Now, making toast is as simple as popping in a few pieces of bread and waiting, making it a quick and nutritious breakfast food.

28. Electron microscope

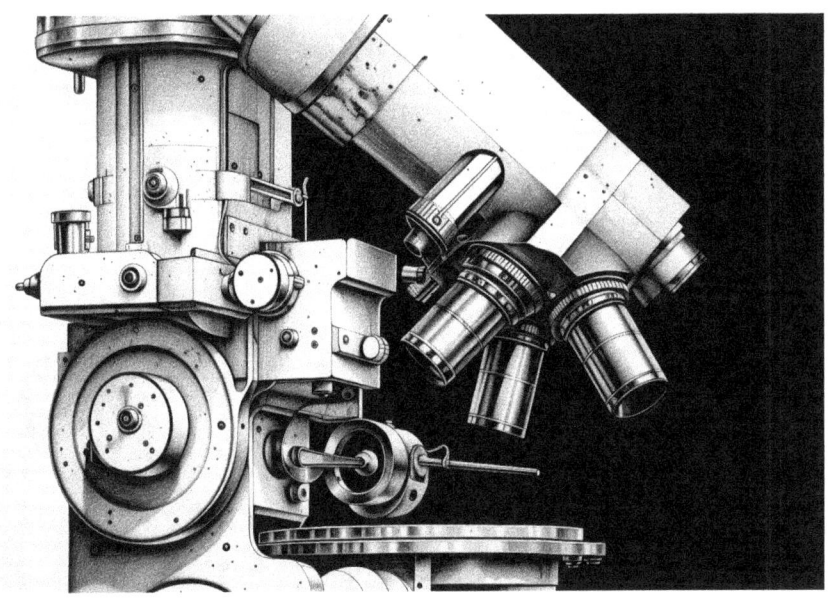

Since the invention of the microscope, society benefited greatly from seeing small things on a larger scale. However, the standard microscope had several limitations, especially in the area of magnification and clarity. The answer to this issue was the creation of the electron microscope, which uses a beam of electrons to illuminate the objects being studied. Several pieces of what would make up the electron microscope were created years before it was invented. It was not until 1928 that Max Knoll and Ernst Ruska developed the device at the Technical University of Berlin. Since then, several types of this microscope have been created. Currently, they are most used for looking at microorganisms and individual cells. This makes them useful for medical diagnostics and industrial quality control, leading to a safer and better world.

29. MRI machine

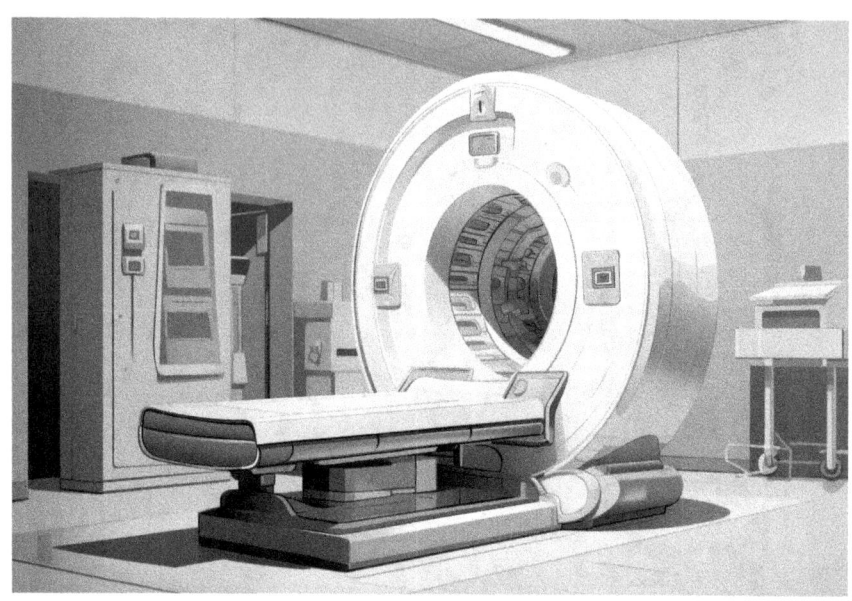

The MRI (magnetic resonance imaging) machine is a standard piece of medical equipment commonly used for diagnostic and research purposes. The device was created in 1960, but its value would not be realized for a few more years. A decade later, the MRI's use in diagnosing various diseases was recognized. The device uses magnets and radio waves to generate images of the inside of a person's body, allowing doctors to see parts that are not visible from the outside. Patients enter a long tube for the images to be taken, and although some find it uncomfortable, it is overall worth it due to its higher levels of clarity when looking at soft tissue. MRIs are used to screen for cancer, diagnose brain conditions, check for heart abnormalities, and perform various other life-saving screenings. Countless lives have been saved due to this device since its invention, and it continues to be one of the most important diagnostic tools in medicine.

30. Prednisone

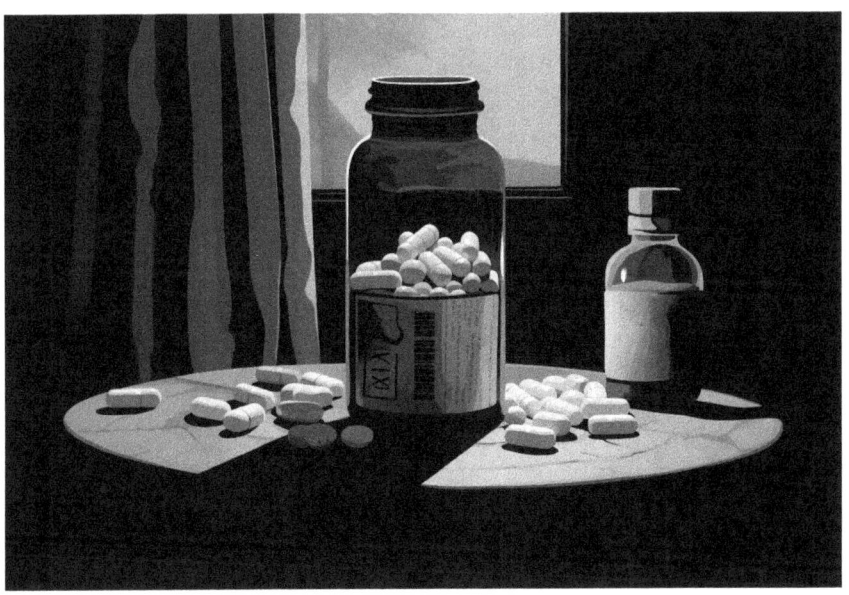

Prednisone is a medication used to stop inflammation in the body and suppress the immune system. It is often referred to as a "steroid" and is most commonly known for its usage in treating upper respiratory infections that are causing inflammatory responses in the body. However, the medication is more important than that. Prednisone has been a life-changing treatment for various illnesses, most of which are auto-immune in nature, such as asthma and arthritis. Currently, it is used to treat a variety of ailments ranging from migraines to Hodgkin's lymphoma. It is also utilized to suppress the immune system following organ transplants to lower the chances that the body will reject the new organ. The drug was created in 1955 by Arthur Nobile and the Schering Corporation. While the list of side effects from long-term usage of this medication concern some, the benefits heavily outweigh the risks for most individuals taking it, and its creation has led to longer, healthier lives for many.

31. Cell phone

When the telephone was initially created, people could only call one another at home, at businesses that allowed usage of their business phone line, or at public phone booths that often cost money. Initially, this was not an issue as previously people were unable to contact each other as efficiently to begin with. Pre-phone life relied on letters, word of mouth, and occasional telegram usage. Yet, in the early 1970s, calls for a more portable option became commonplace. In 1973, Martin Cooper invented the first mobile phone, which he demonstrated to the public. However, the mobile phone could not even be used until the launch of the first mobile network in 1979. In 1983, the product finally became commercially available. Since then, mobile phone usage has grown rapidly, allowing people to talk from anywhere in the world. In addition, advancements have been made, allowing for more compact devices with longer battery life and more abilities. Although modern cell phones are nothing like these early models, they all still maintain the ability to make calls no matter the user's location.

32. X-ray machine

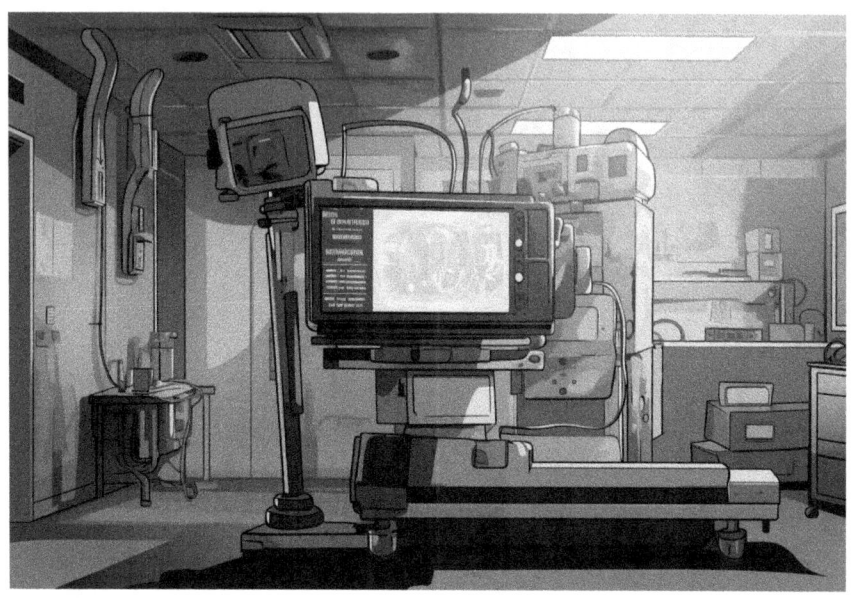

X-ray machines are devices created from two parts: an X-ray generator and an X-ray detector. These machines have a variety of uses, most notably in medical and security settings. X-rays were discovered by accident in 1895 by scientist Wilhelm Conrad Rontgen. He found that the rays could pass through many different types of material, including human bodies. This led to their usage in diagnosis, starting with medics using them to find bullets inside people during wartime. In modern medicine, X-rays are used by radiologists to diagnose various ailments. They are most known for being used to check for broken bones, but they are also helpful for certain kinds of cancer, lung conditions such as pneumonia, and bowel conditions such as bowel obstructions. Security guards may use a similar X-ray device to check for objects a person may be hiding, allowing them to confiscate any concerning items before a person enters a secured location. Both medical and security usage of this device has helped society become a safer place.

33. Nitroglycerin

Nitroglycerin is a unique substance that has been extremely useful as both an explosive and a medication. It was created by Ascario Sobrero in 1847, and although he warned about its power, it quickly became a popular explosive. The compound was a great help and hindrance during its early days, as it allowed mining and railroad creation to happen quickly, but it also caused many tragedies due to improper use and storage. William Murrell changed how we use the compound in 1878, finding it helpful when treating angina pectoris (a type of heart-related chest pain). When taken into the body, nitroglycerin creates nitric oxide, which helps with blood pressure and blood vessel dilation. Over time, more nitrates with similar effects were discovered, providing a new treatment route for heart conditions. These medications allow people with angina pectoris and some types of heart failure to enjoy life and stay active despite their conditions.

34. Bluetooth

Bluetooth devices have a built-in chip that emits and receives radio waves, allowing them to connect to each other without the need for wires or cables. They work via high-frequency radio waves. This type of wireless communication was invented in 1989 by Ericsson Mobile worker Nils Rydbeck, and it rapidly gained traction as more uses for the technology were discovered. Initially, Bluetooth technology was mainly used to connect phones to special headsets that allowed people to talk on the phone without using their hands. Soon, it was also used to enable phones to connect to car speaker systems. As technology advances, more applications for Bluetooth are found, and today, it is used to connect phones to speakers, cameras, and even locking systems on doors. Most gaming consoles also use the technology to connect controllers to gaming systems. Bluetooth technology will likely advance as the need for more short-distance communication between household devices grows.

35. DNA fingerprinting

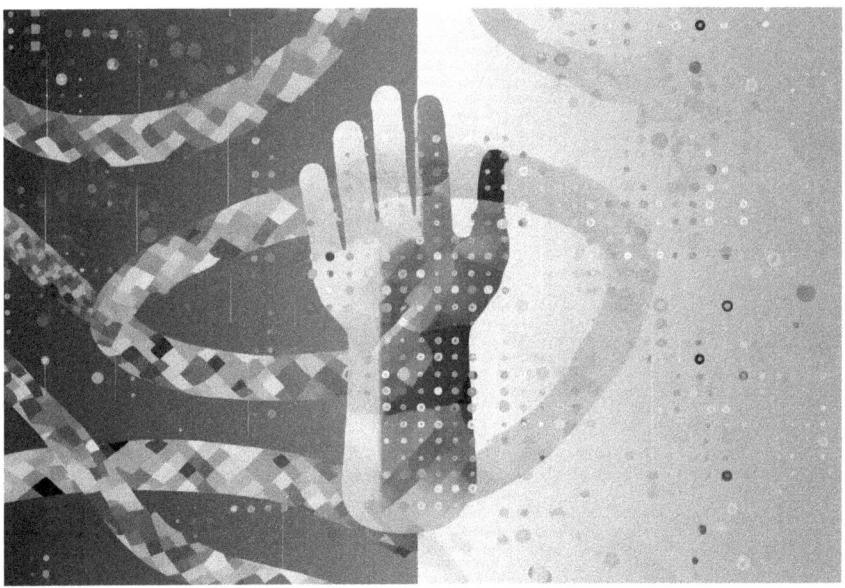

DNA fingerprinting is a process that aids investigators in identifying potential criminals by comparing the DNA of a sample taken from a person to the DNA of a sample taken from a crime scene. It also can be used for genealogy and paternity testing. DNA, or deoxyribonucleic acid, is the building block of life. All organic materials are composed of DNA, which consists of molecules called polymers intertwined in a twisting, ladder-like shape known as a double helix. These molecules comprise special cells called nucleotides that come in four types: adenine, cytosine, guanine, and thymine. The patterns created by these four nucleotides differ depending on where the DNA comes from. DNA profiling is composed of extracting DNA from samples and then comparing the nucleotide patterns to determine whether they match. The process was first discovered in 1983 by Jeffrey Glassburg. Since then, it has been used to identify many criminals, such as Joseph James DeAngelo, also known as the Golden State Killer.

Improvements in technology have made the process faster and more accurate, with even more improvements to be expected in the future.

36. Wi-Fi

Wi-Fi is a method of wirelessly accessing the Internet via a router or access point and radio waves. It is the wireless sibling to Ethernet, which works similarly but requires devices to be plugged in to access the Internet. The idea was first tested in 1992 via Australia's Commonwealth Scientific and Industrial Research Organization. The early version of Wi-Fi was released in 1997, but it did not gain popularity until 1999 when Apple's laptop series, the iBook, began to offer connectivity via the product. Slowly, Wi-Fi began to become available on more products and grew in popularity. Now almost all laptops and smartphones have the ability to use Wi-Fi to access the Internet. In addition, most gaming consoles also share the ability. This has made the Internet easily accessible for many and has even allowed individuals to use their personal devices to access public Internet services, such as those found in public libraries. Increasing speeds and increases in efficiency are continuously being sought after, leading Wi-Fi to be an ever-expanding concept.

37. Hypodermic syringe

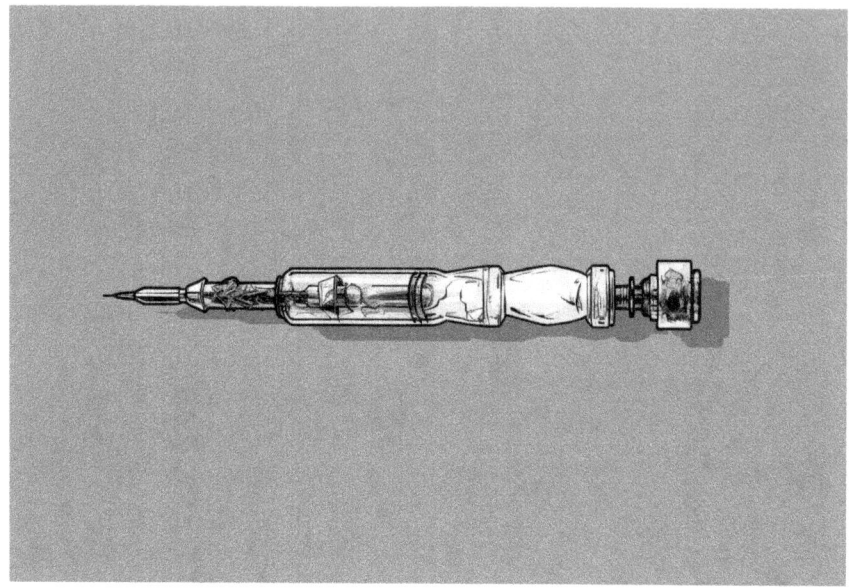

Hypodermic syringes consist of a cylindrical tube to hold liquids, a plunger to push fluids forward, and a hollow needle to deliver liquids into the human body. These devices allow for medicine's safe, sterile delivery into the skin, muscles, blood vessels, and fatty tissue. The first documented attempt at using a hypodermic syringe was by Christopher Wren in 1656, when he used it to experiment on dogs. Animal bladders acted as the syringe, while goose quills were used as rudimentary needles. These experiments often lead to the animal's death, causing the technique to be ignored for the next two centuries. Finally, in 1851, Alexander Wood created the all-glass syringe leading to a safe, effective way of giving injections. This allowed for injections to grow in popularity as physicians began to use them to administer medicine quickly and in smaller dosages. The following significant change, the disposable hypodermic needle, was invented in the 1950s, ensuring additional cleanliness in using needles in medicine. Since then, various minor advancements and variations have been made to the device. As more discoveries are made, the hypodermic needle will continue to undergo changes.

38. GPS

The GPS, or global positioning system, is a system that uses satellites and radio waves to determine one's location. Known initially as Navstar GPS, the United States government launched the project in 1973 to correct issues that previous similar systems dealt with. The system works by bouncing radio waves back and forth from a GPS device on Earth. These waves bounce back on satellites, which help determine the device's location. The United States Space Force operates the system, but it has been available for civilian use since the 1980s. While the original purpose of GPS was to aid in government and military expeditions, the GPS has become a popular navigation tool for civilians. Window-mounted GPS systems became commonplace in vehicles in the early 2000s, only later replaced by vehicles with built-in GPS systems. In addition, modern smartphones are equipped with this technology, allowing easy navigation for most of the Western world.

39. USB drive

USB drives are devices that allow one to store data and easily erase it when it is no longer needed. They are small and portable, making them an easy way to transport information. The device was first created by M-Systems, a company from Israel, in 1999. Early flash drives could only hold small amounts of data and often took a long time to upload and download documents. Over time, this tool has gotten faster, and the amount of information it can hold has grown significantly. While many individuals choose to use cloud storage systems, the USB is still sometimes preferred due to its high degree of security, its compatibility with encryption and biometrics, and its use in running applications without needing to install them on a physical computer. They are generally considered safer than cloud storage, leading to a high usage rate by law enforcement and government agencies. Improvements in size, speed, and storage are still being made.

40. Thermometer

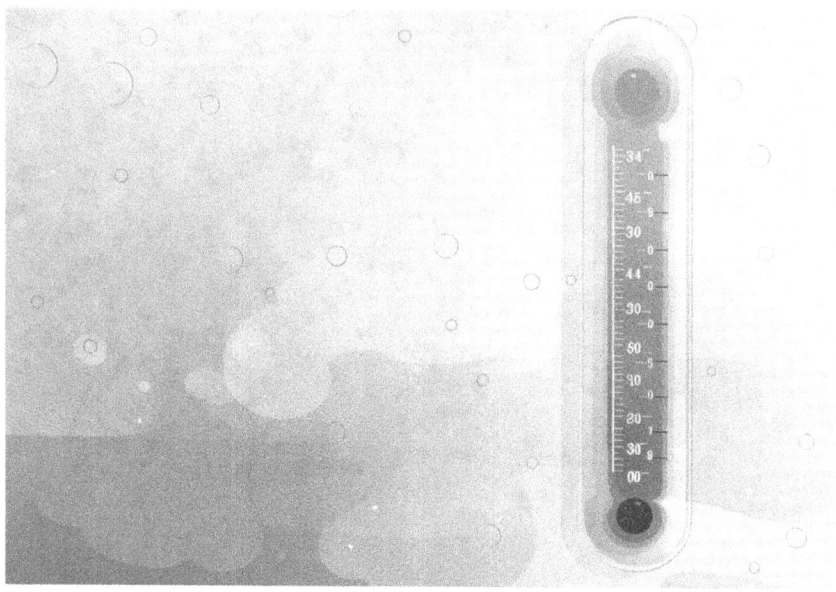

A thermometer is a device used to tell the temperature of an object or being. Many of us are familiar with digital thermometers that can quickly tell whether one has a fever. However, originally most thermometers were made from two simple materials: glass and mercury. When mercury is heated, it turns into a liquid and expands. When encased in a tube, the mercury's expansion correlates to the heat level it absorbs. Early thermometers used water and brandy instead of mercury, making readings less accurate. It wasn't until 1714 that Daniel Gabriel Fahrenheit invented the mercury thermometer and created the scale that one day would bear his name. Later, Anders Celcius would similarly invent the Celcius scale. Together, these two men made it possible to accurately determine the temperature of living beings and that of various liquids. This allowed medicine to become more efficient and additionally has led to safer cooking practices. Today, thermometers are often digital and do not contain the mercury and glass that were once common.

Did You Know?

Bioluminescence is the awe-inspiring phenomenon where living organisms produce and emit light, creating a mystical glow in various environments on Earth. This natural illumination has fascinated scientists and nature enthusiasts, shedding light (pun intended) on the marvels of evolution.

Delve into the luminous world of bioluminescence:

• Ocean's Depths: Most bioluminescent organisms reside in the ocean, especially in its darkest and deepest parts. Creatures like anglerfish use this glow to attract prey, while others use it to ward off predators or find mates.

• Land and Sky Wonders: Fireflies are among the most iconic land-based bioluminescent creatures. Their enchanting evening dances are mating rituals, with each species having its unique flashing pattern. Certain fungi emit a greenish glow in caves, leading to the spectacle known as "foxfire."

• Chemical Reaction: At the heart of bioluminescence is a chemical reaction. When the molecule luciferin reacts with oxygen, aided by the enzyme luciferase, it produces a radiant glow.

• A Light in Medicine: The science behind bioluminescence is now being harnessed in medical research. By tagging cells with the genes that produce this light, researchers can track diseases like cancer and monitor how treatments work in real-time.

Bioluminescence is a radiant testament to nature's ability to adapt and innovate. From the depths of the oceans to the labs of cutting-edge research, this glow continues to illuminate mysteries waiting to be explored.

41. Copernican Theory

Copernican Theory, also known as Copernican heliocentrism, is the scientifically validated belief that the planets revolve around the Sun. Before 1543, most people believed that the planets and the Sun revolved around the Earth. This was called the geocentric model. Nicolaus Copernicus challenged this by publishing his theory stating that the Earth and several other planets revolve around the Sun. The Earth moves in three different ways (daily rotation, annual revolution, and axis tilting); planets seemingly moving in reverse is actually due to Earth's movements, and the Earth is closer to the Sun than the Sun is to the other stars. Overall, Copernicus' theory was far more accurate than the geocentric model. While some of the theory has been disproven, such as the Earth's axial tilt changing daily, the general idea remains true. The Earth and the other planets of our solar system travel around the Sun.

42. Central heating

Before central heating was invented, households were forced to heat each room of the house individually. Fireplaces and stoves were used to keep rooms warm, but this heat was rarely able to travel throughout an entire building. This made keeping an entire house warm on a cold winter day difficult. Central heating takes the heat created by a single heat source and disperses it throughout various locations. This is usually done via heating ducts or pipes. The first example of central heating can be found in ancient Greece and Rome. Empty spaces and pipes were placed in the floor system and connected to where a fire would be lit. This allowed the warmth from the fire to spread across buildings. Modern examples of central heating now use furnaces, boilers, and water heaters to produce heat instead of fire. This allows entire houses to be heated via steam, water, or electricity. This saves us plenty of time that would have been spent making fires and tending to them in the past.

43. Gregorian calendar

The Gregorian calendar, our prevailing arbiter of time, isn't merely a tool for marking days—it represents humanity's intricate dance with the cosmos, our attempt to align earthly rhythms with celestial cycles. Instituted by Pope Gregory XIII in 1582, this calendar emerged to realign the date of the Christian celebration of Easter with the spring equinox, correcting the drift caused by the Julian calendar's imprecise calculation of leap years. In the Julian system, every fourth year was a leap year. But this added slightly too many leap days over the centuries. The Gregorian solution was elegant: while maintaining the rule that years divisible by four would be leap years, a new caveat was introduced. Centurial years, like 1700 or 1800, would be leap years only if they were divisible by 400. Hence, while 1600 and 2000 were leap years, 1700, 1800, and 1900 were not. To instate the calendar, a one-time correction was made in October 1582 by "erasing" ten days. Overnight, the 4th of October transformed into the 15th. Its global acceptance, however, was staggered. Catholic nations were early adopters, but Protestant and Orthodox regions, wary of papal decrees, took longer, some even centuries, to transition. Today, the Gregorian calendar's ubiquity in business, science, and daily affairs speaks volumes about its precision and significance. While traditional calendars with lunar or lunisolar bases still guide cultural and religious events in many regions, the Gregorian system stands as the civil standard—a testament to our shared quest for temporal accuracy and unity.

44. Pacemaker

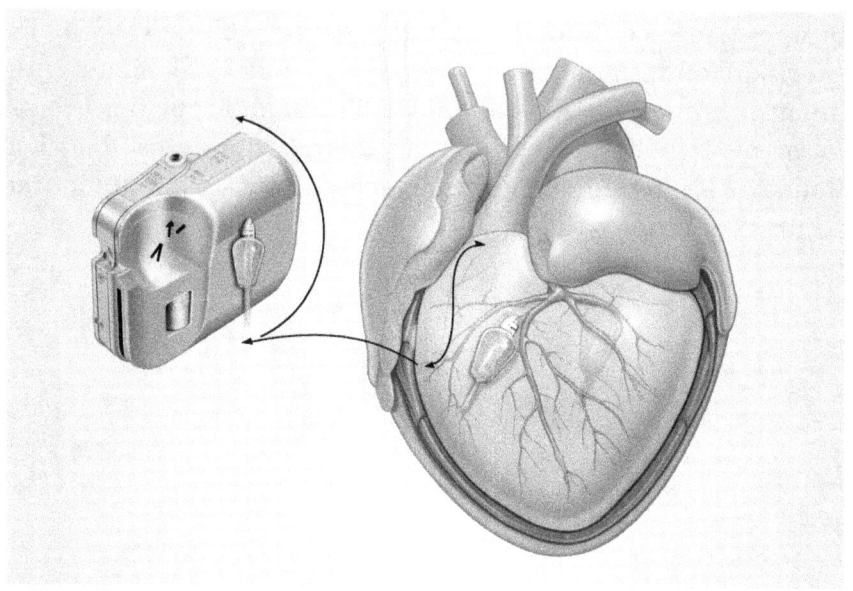

Sometimes, people have issues with the pace at that their heart beats. When somebody's heart beats too slowly, a device called a pacemaker may help the heart beat at a better pace. These devices send electrical impulses to various parts of the heart, causing them to contract. Early pacemakers had to be worn on the outside of the body. A 1958 model consisted of an external mechanism held inside a box and a series of wires and electrodes that pass through the patient's skin to stimulate the heart directly. After this, advancements were rapidly made in pursuit of a device that was efficient, long-lasting, and convenient. Lithium batteries and special metal casings proved to be some of the most valuable changes made to pacemakers. These changes help them last longer and also help them avoid damage while inside the human body. Overall, these devices can add years to the lives of those who wear them, making them important to humankind.

45. Online streaming

For a long time, individuals had to access media via physical copies bought in stores or from downloads off of the Internet. Music was available through cassette tapes, CDs, and mp3 downloads. Movies and television shows could be bought via VHS or DVD or accessed via a cable or satellite dish subscription. This limited the amount of media one could access and made accessing large amounts of media expensive. This changed with the invention of online streaming. Streaming refers to media that is available continuously without download or ownership. YouTube was one of the first streaming platforms to become popular, with user-created content accessible to anyone. Eventually, other streaming services appeared. Today, there are a large amount of these services available. Some cater to music, such as Apple Music and Pandora. Others focus on television and movies, such as Netflix and Hulu. These services have made media cheap and easy to access. Without them, our ability to watch and listen to media would still be extremely limited.

46. Manufactured insulin

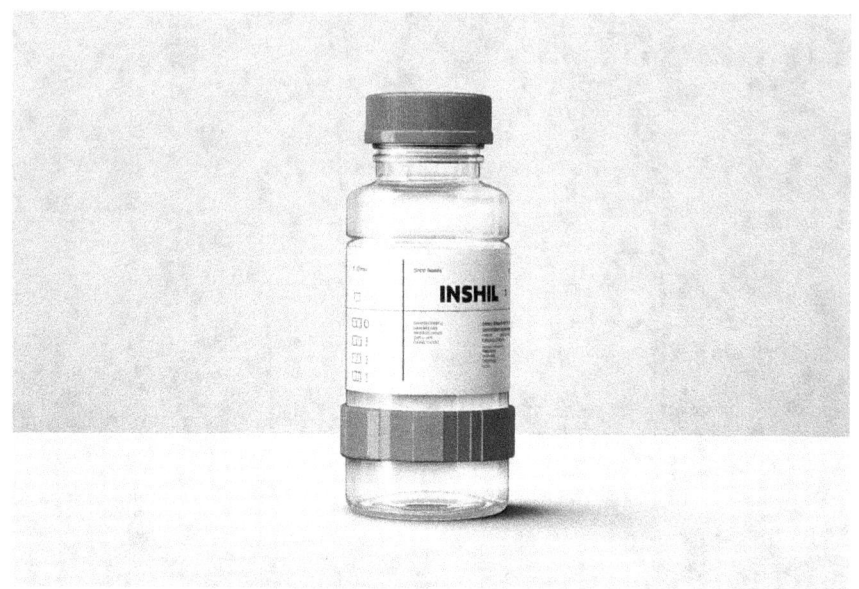

Diabetes is known as a serious but manageable condition. However, this was not always the case. For many years people with diabetes had a shortened life expectancy, and there was not much that could be done to lessen the effects of the disease. In 1922, this changed forever as Frederick Banting and Charles Best treated a young teenager named Leonard Thompson with insulin derived from cattle. The treatment successfully lowered Thompson's blood sugar, leading to the utilization of cattle-derived insulin to treat diabetics. However, not all patients reacted positively to the insulin, as many were allergic. In 1978, this changed with the creation of synthetic insulin, which mimicked the insulin naturally produced by the human body. This new "human" insulin was slowly experimented on, and even more advancements were made. Scientists were able to create insulin that released more slowly and lasted longer. This has led to longer, better lives for diabetic patients.

47. Internal combustion engine

For many years, travel relied on literal horsepower or manpower. This caused trips to be long and tedious. Even with the invention of the steam engine, travel was still slow and difficult for most. This changed with the invention and popularity of the internal combustion engine, which uses the burning and expansion of gasses to move pistons to generate power. Thomas Newcomen invented this engine in the 1700s, but this model was not ready for public use. It wasn't until the 1900s that the combustion engine became efficient enough for regular usage. Jean-Joseph Etienne Lenoir created a proper working model in 1859, which was used as a framework for the popular models of the 1900s. Advances in thermodynamics and the invention of three combustion sources (carburation, hot bulb vaporization, and the diesel engine) followed. Without these advancements, the modern automobile industry would not exist.

48. Cochlear prosthetics

Cochlear prosthetics are a type of device that helps individuals with a specific kind of hearing impairment. These prosthetics allow some deaf and hard-of-hearing individuals to hear efficiently. Specifically, they work on individuals with sensorineural hearing loss caused by inner ear issues or issues with the internal organs of the ear. The device electrically stimulates the auditory nerve instead of forcing the individual to rely on simple, acoustic hearing. More precisely, it stimulates a specific nerve found in the cochlea. André Djourno and Charles Eyriès invented the first model in 1957. Since then, steady advancements have been made, with Adam Kissiah creating the modern version in 1977. This device has allowed many people with hearing impairments to live normal lives, greatly enhancing their ability to hear and communicate, leading to a higher quality of life.

49. Morphine

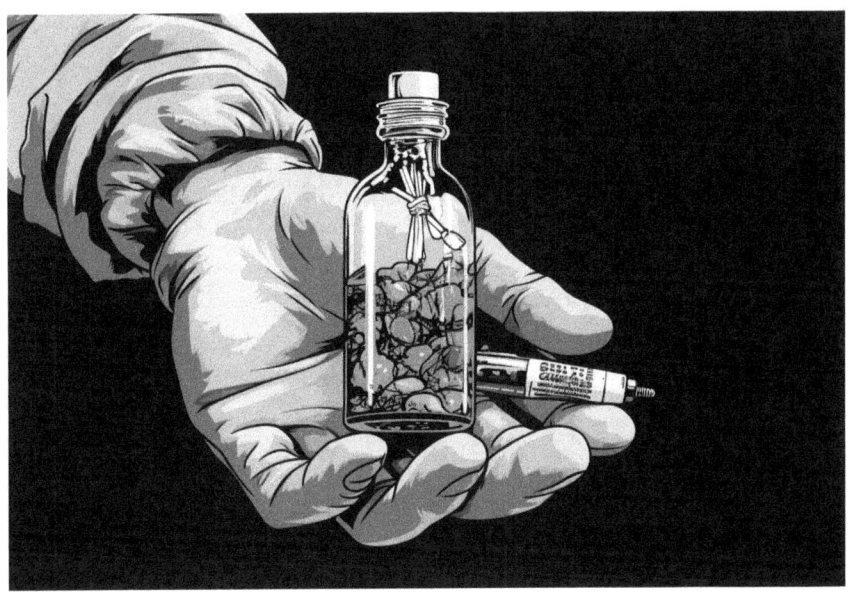

While opioids have gained a negative reputation in recent years due to overuse and addiction, they have been beneficial inventions in the medical field. Central to this tale is morphine, a discovery that heralded a new era in pain management. Friedrich Seturner extracted the primary alkaloid from the opium poppy plant in 1804, initiating experiments on himself and other creatures. Morphine is six times stronger than its predecessor, opium, leading to its adoption by the medical field in 1817. It is used to treat pain in various situations, including pain due to sudden injury and chronic illness. In addition, it can treat feelings of breathlessness in a safe, controlled manner. It is a critical medicine for end-of-life care, as it aids in keeping patients comfortable and relaxed. In addition, later opioids all stem from the study of morphine, meaning we would not have access to many other substances we rely on without the invention of this particular medicine.

50. Dissolvable sutures

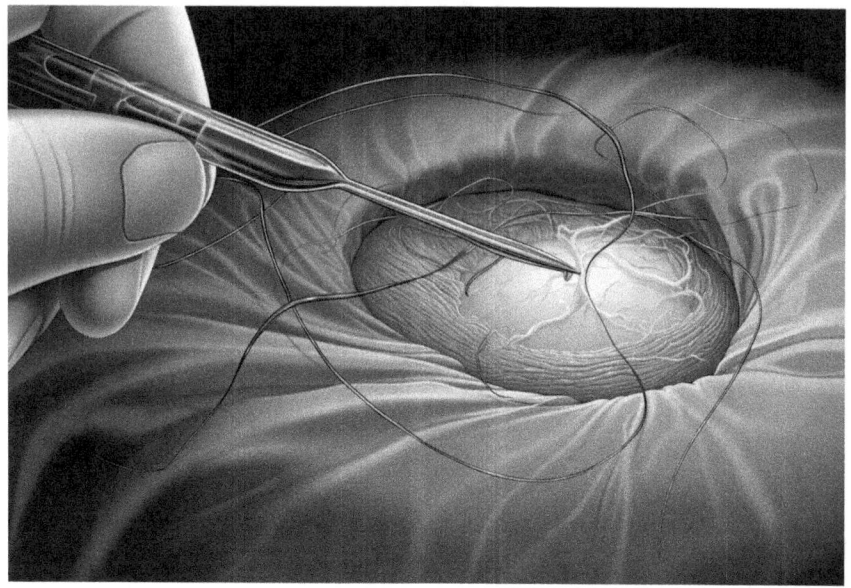

Surgery's longstanding reliance on sutures posed a unique challenge: the eventual need to revisit and remove them. This prompted the innovation of dissolvable sutures, a groundbreaking development that eliminated the often cumbersome post-operative suture removal process. These self-resolving threads, most commonly employed for internal surgeries, negate the intricate task of extracting sutures from the body's inner recesses. Moreover, they're invaluable for patients who, for various reasons, might not revisit the clinic for stitch removal. This not only mitigates potential complications from unsanctioned at-home extractions but also the risks associated with retaining non-dissolvable sutures indefinitely. Available in both natural and synthetic variants, dissolvable sutures, while not universally applicable, have significantly enhanced post-operative care, minimizing both patient discomfort and medical follow-up demands.

51. Laser

The laser, which stands for "light amplification by stimulated emission of radiation," has changed medical science and manufacturing since its invention in 1959 by Gordon Gould. Interestingly, lasers were invented without a specific purpose in mind. This allowed them to gain popularity in various fields, including the medical field, consumer electronics, information technology, and even the military. This led to several new technologies, such as fiber-optic communication, barcode scanners, and laser printers. Laser surgery also grew in popularity over time, with the device being used to do everything, from removing blemishes to breaking down kidney stones. The military has invented another use for lasers by creating high-energy weapons that harness the power of a laser into a powerful tool. Today, new uses for the laser are still being discovered. The invention remains useful everywhere, helping humanity from the classroom to the hospital and even to the manufacturing plant.

52. Microwave oven

Can you imagine a world where the fastest cooking device available is a convection oven? This was the reality for people who lived before 1945. In 1945, Percy Spencer invented the microwave oven, a metal box that could cook food using electromagnetic radiation. This newfound way of cooking relied on the way that these radioactive waves caused the molecules and items of food to suddenly move faster, causing the food to become warmer quickly. Eventually, advancements were made that made the microwave oven even more efficient. One such advancement was that of the rotating turntable. This ensured that food was cooked evenly on all sides. Early microwave ovens were huge and were only available for commercial use. This changed in the 1970s when smaller models were made for at-home use. It was during this time that the average family was able to afford the product. Since then, the microwave oven has grown in popularity to the point where most households use one regularly.

53. Clock

Imagine having to tell time using only the sun and a shadow. Before clocks, sundials were the primary way of telling time, making it difficult to tell time in certain weather and at night. Archimedes was one of the first individuals to create something resembling modern-day clocks. He used water, weight systems, ropes, and gears to produce a water clock that could act as an astronomical clock and an hourly clock. However, the clock as we know it today was not invented until 1511 when a locksmith named Peter Henlien invented the first world spring-driven clock. This changed the way we view time. Precision measurements of hours, minutes, and seconds allowed people to follow more specific schedules and made appointment settings easier. In addition, clockmaking became an art form, and clocks became essential pieces of furniture in the home. Over time, advancements were made. Digital clocks now exist that do not rely on mechanical gears. Furthermore, alarm clocks have also been created to notify an individual when it is a particular time. Timekeeping has never been easier than it is now, thanks to these devices.

54. Concrete

Concrete is a mixture of solid particles and liquid cement that is used in construction. This mixture forms a thick liquid that can be poured into various molds and left to harden. The resulting material is hard and sturdy. Concrete has existed in various forms since ancient civilizations. Early concrete was made primarily with a substance called calcium oxide, also known as hydraulic lime. Later materials included volcanic ash, pozzolanic ash, and pumice. Currently, Portland cement is the primary material used and primarily consists of hydraulic lime. Concrete is popular as a building material for a variety of reasons including its extreme durability, its fire-resistant tendencies, and the fact that it actually grows in strength over time. In addition, the invention of reinforced concrete has increased the material's usefulness. Concrete is strong when compressed, but brittle when dealing with tension. Reinforced concrete uses iron cables, wires, and rods to add additional strength to the structures. This allows concrete to be used in a wider variety of construction projects.

55. Compact disc

The compact disc, or CD as it's more commonly known, is a storage device co-invented by the companies of Phillips and Sony to create a format for storing digital music files. The CD was released in 1982, and later a sister format called the CD-ROM was released, which was used to store files other than music. These discs could store more data than the storage devices before them, such as the cassette tape. This also made music more portable, allowing people to bring their favorite music wherever they went. Radio DJs could switch songs more quickly, and amateur artists could easily burn their music onto CDs to hand out as demos. The discs also enabled the incorporation of customized artwork, and designs could be added directly to the disc if desired. Editing these discs was also simple through a computer, allowing for personalized adjustments. Overall, the compact disc made music easy to manage and carry.

56. Fire extinguisher

While many people will never use a fire extinguisher in their lifetimes, everyone should know the value of the device. Fire extinguishers are tools that are meant to put out dangerous fires. They contain chemicals specifically formulated to quickly put out a flame with minimal hazard to the user. Ambrose Godfrey invented the first fire extinguisher in 1723, using a fire-extinguishing liquid and gunpowder to blow the liquid over the fire. Its efficacy was recorded in contemporary newspapers. Soon, smaller versions of the device emerged, employing compressed air for liquid deployment instead of gunpowder. Later models used water and aluminum sulfate to put out flames. Some odd advancements led to the invention of fire grenades, which were glass containers with extinguishing liquids meant to be thrown at fires. Halon is currently one of the more common materials used in these devices, but it is being slowly removed due to environmental concerns. Overall, the fire extinguisher has saved many lives, and advancements in the device are made regularly.

57. Cleats

Cleats are shoes that have special soles designed to provide a better grip on certain surfaces. These soles are fitted with studs that help grip slippery surfaces. The first instance of this kind of shoe can be traced back to ancient Rome. A type of sandal boot was invented called caligae, which had special studs on the bottom to provide additional traction. Soldiers often wore these shoes to ensure proper footing in battle. However, modern cleats were not invented until the 1500s. King Henry VIII is documented as having one of these early pairs of cleats, with Isaac Ali cited as the shoemaker. In the 1800s, football grew in popularity, and the need for durable cleats grew rapidly. Vulcanized rubber was created to add extra durability to the shoe. Soon, other sports began to adopt the cleat. Baseball and American football require its use to prevent injury. Truly, cleats have aided in injury prevention throughout history and continue to be an important piece of sporting equipment.

58. Washing machine

The washing machine revolutionized the way we do laundry. Before the laundry machine was invented, garments had to be hand washed. This process involved carrying water to a location, dipping clothes in soapy water, agitating the clothes by hand, and then rinsing the clothes out with fresh water. This task was labor-intensive and time-consuming. The washing machine was created in 1937 by Bendix Home Appliances. These machines closely resembled modern washing machines, although they were costly. Progress continued, and although the device remained costly, its popularity soared during the 1950s. The impact made by this machine is much more significant than expected, as it had a drastic effect on women. Washing clothes was a task that women had to undergo regularly. The creation of this machine took away the long hours of labor women had to undergo when doing laundry, giving them more free time and aiding them in slowly escaping domestic servitude.

59. Dishwasher

The quest for mechanized dishwashing dates back to 1850 when Joel Houghton patented a wooden device with a hand-turned wheel to splash water on dishes. Yet, this primitive contraption was just the beginning. In 1887, Josephine Cochrane, a socialite tired of her china being chipped by the help, showcased her invention at the 1893 World's Columbian Exposition in Chicago. Her design, which employed water jets and wire racks to hold the dishes, is conceptually closest to the modern dishwasher. Notably, Cochrane's machines were initially marketed to restaurants and hotels, rather than households. The journey of the dishwasher from a luxury item to a household staple is equally compelling. William Howard Livens' 1924 design introduced many elements familiar today, but it was the post-World War II economic prosperity that spurred its domestic popularity. Coupled with evolving societal dynamics, like the rise of dual-income households and changing gender roles, the demand for time-saving appliances grew. By the 1970s, the dishwasher wasn't just about cleaning dishes—it was a symbol of modern convenience and progressive domesticity. Today's dishwashers are not only efficient but are also designed with eco-conscious features, ensuring minimal water and energy consumption, reflecting society's growing environmental awareness.

60. CT machine

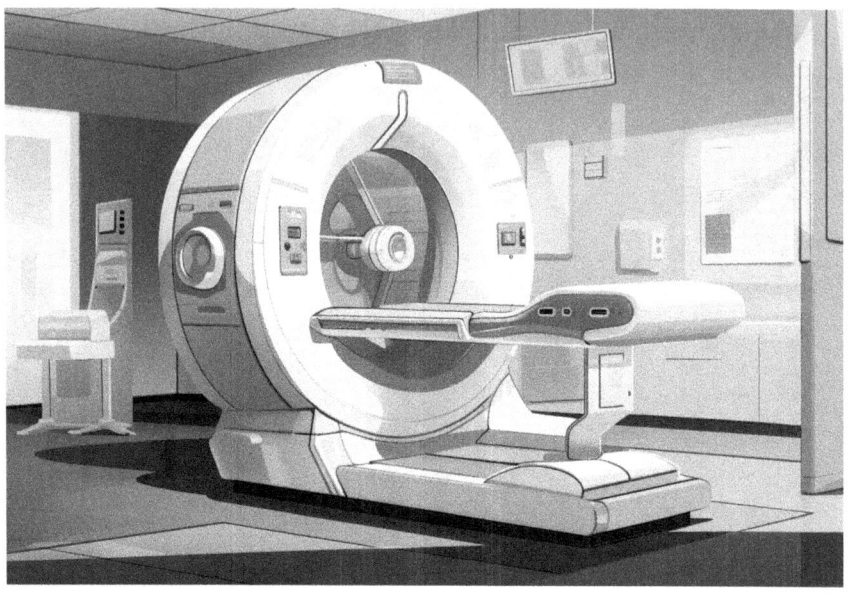

The CT machine, also known as the computed tomography machine, is a medical device used to diagnose certain illnesses and injuries. It uses radiation to look inside the human body to diagnose issues that cannot be seen from the outside. The first usable CT machine was created by Godfrey Hounsfield in 1972. The device is enormous and requires the usage of an X-ray. It creates a picture from the raw data called a sinogram, which must be combined to form a tomographic reconstruction. This can show any abnormal findings and abnormal densities of expected structures. Radioactive contrast can be added if blood vessels need to be seen, as regular usage of the machine makes them difficult to separate from the other tissue. The CT machine has a variety of advantages over other methods of diagnosis. First of all, it creates a more precise image than several other types of common scanners. Second, it can replace invasive procedures requiring doctors to enter the human body to diagnose.

Did You Know?

The concept known as the "butterfly effect" posits that small changes in a system can lead to dramatic differences in outcome. The name comes from the idea that the flap of a butterfly's wings in Brazil could set off a tornado in Texas, emphasizing the interconnectedness and sensitivity of complex systems.

This notion has taken root not just in meteorology, where it originated, but in fields as varied as finance, philosophy, and popular culture:

• Chaos Theory: The butterfly effect is a fundamental idea within chaos theory, a branch of mathematics that deals with systems that appear to be disordered or random but are actually deterministic in nature.

• Philosophy: Philosophers have pondered the implications of the butterfly effect, especially when it comes to the concepts of fate, destiny, and free will.

• Economics: Financial markets can be significantly affected by seemingly minor news or events, leading to significant economic shifts. This sensitivity is often examined in the light of the butterfly effect.

Understanding the butterfly effect reminds us of the intricate connections underpinning our world, reinforcing that even our most minor actions can have wide-reaching ramifications.

61. DNA sequencers

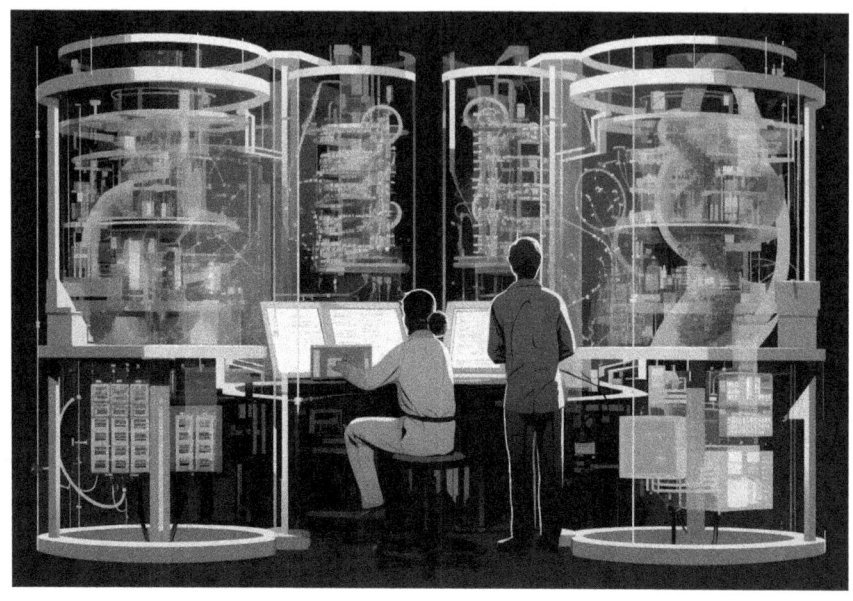

Genetic sequencing, also known as DNA sequencing, involves the study and understanding of the patterns of DNA and the meaning of these patterns. Genetic sequencing specifically analyzes the four different kinds of nucleotides found in DNA: adenine, guanine, cytosine, and thymine. For a very long time, this process was extremely tedious and required a lot of manual work, including extraction in analysis. Despite the efforts needed to sequence DNA, it became an essential job due to its use in virology and medical science. In 1987, Lloyd M. Smith created a device that did most of the work required without human intervention. Later, the Human Genome Project began the second generation of these devices, making them more affordable and significantly faster at sequencing DNA. Recently, a third generation has been developed to allow longer strands of DNA to be processed at one time. This has the potential to make the process even faster, making diagnosis and research less time-consuming.

62. Porcelain veneers

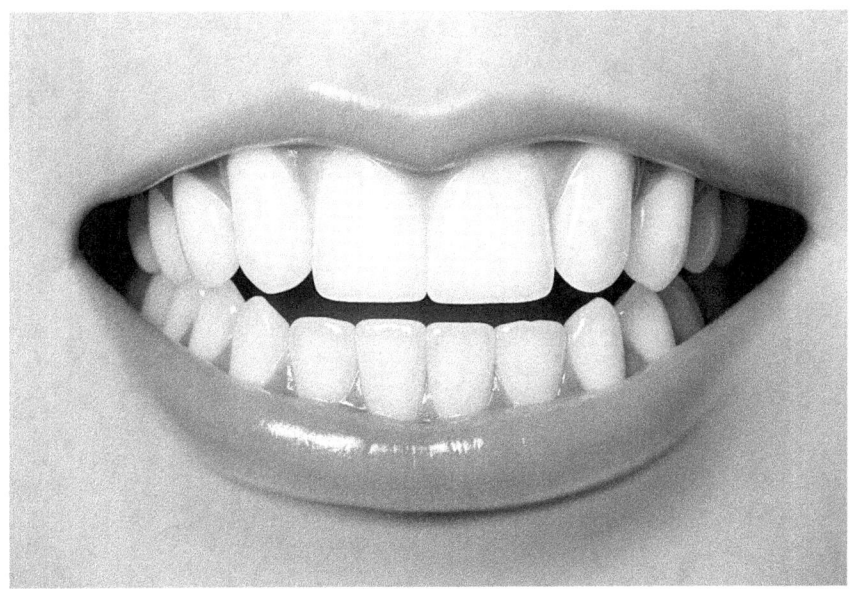

Have you ever heard of something called porcelain veneers? Porcelain veneers are a treatment option for various dental issues that do not require the patient to have their teeth removed. Instead, the veneers are placed over the patient's original teeth to protect them and prevent further damage. Veneers were invented in 1928 as a temporary way to change the appearance of one's teeth by a dentist named Charles Pincus. However, it was not until 1982 that dentists could find a way to permanently bond veneers to a person's teeth in a safe and long-lasting manner. Veneers do not last forever and must be replaced every ten to thirty years. Despite this, they are an excellent option for individuals with unhealthy teeth who do not want to deal with the pain and struggles of wearing dentures. Once the veneers are installed, the patient does not have to worry about them until they need to be replaced again.

63. Albuterol sulfate

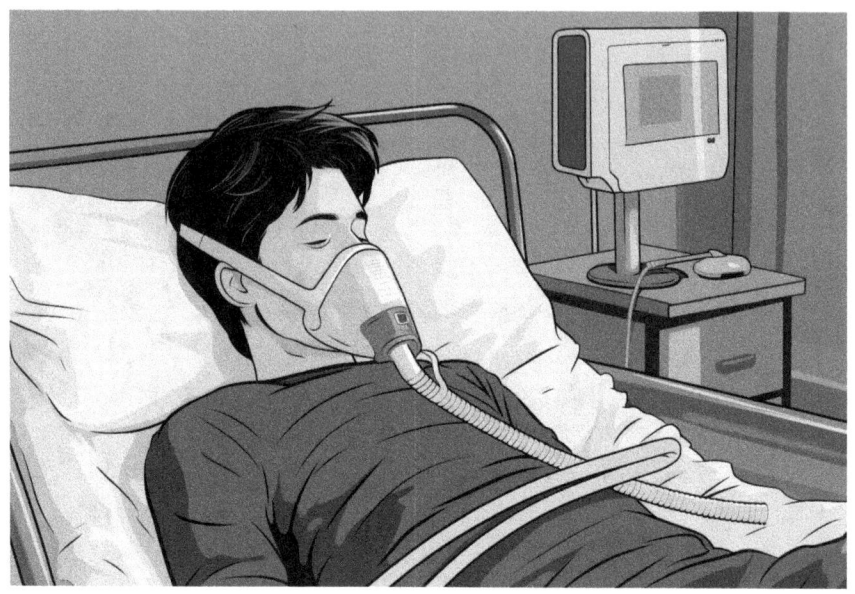

Albuterol sulfate, also known as salbutamol, is a medication used to treat bronchospasm and asthma attacks. This medication was discovered in 1966 by David Jack and was available to the general public by 1969. The drug is a β2 adrenergic receptor agonist, which causes the body's smooth muscles to relax. When inhaled, it specifically works on the lungs. This has led to the drug's popularity as a quick-acting reliever medication for all types of asthma, bronchospasm due to infection, and chronic obstructive pulmonary disease. The drug has saved many lives since its invention, being the first line of treatment in emergency situations involving lung constriction. Without it, many asthmatics would die. Albuterol sulfate comes as an inhaler, a nebulizer solution, a pill, a drinkable liquid, and an intravenous injection. All forms are effective in treating bronchospasm. When paired with a maintenance medication, albuterol sulfate is one of the primary ingredients in creating an effective asthma action plan. Without it, maintaining asthma and chronic obstructive pulmonary disease would be difficult, if not impossible.

64. Flush toilet

Can you imagine going to the bathroom and having to manually dispose of your own waste? This is something that many people had to do before the invention of the flush toilet. Flush toilets allow people to use the bathroom and then flush their waste into the local sewage system via pipes and water. This sewage is then treated with chemicals that make it safer, and afterward, it is stored away from the general public via underground systems. The flush toilet was invented in 1775 by a man named Alexander Cumming. The water in these toilets not only allows for easy flushing and waste removal but also protects users from harmful sewer gasses. Before this, people would use dry toilets, which would collect waste in bins that had to be emptied by hand. Fancier variations allowed for the freezing or burning of waste instead. However, all posed health risks due to toxic gasses and bacteria being released during removal. Thus, the flush toilet has helped humanity stay safe and sanitary since its invention.

65. Cardiac defibrillators

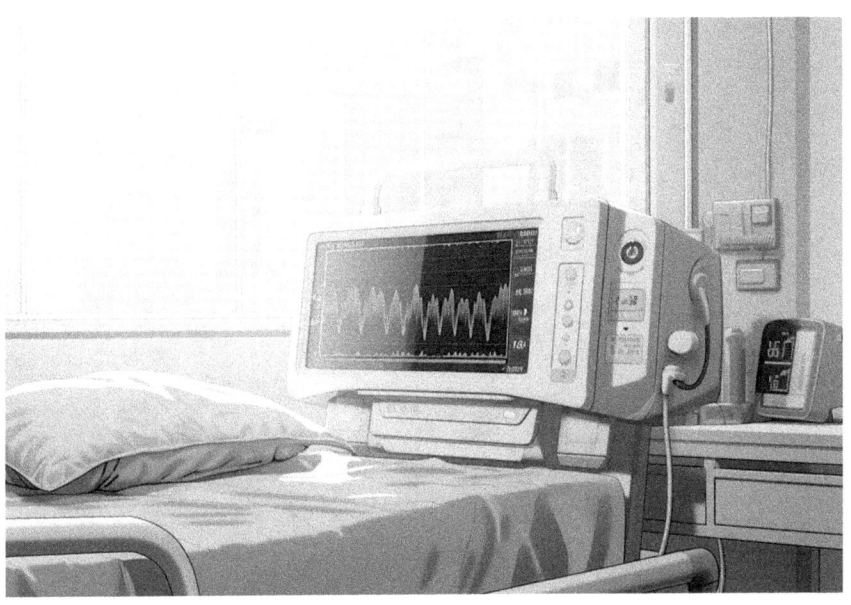

Many people can recall scenes in movies where doctors yell "clear" and place two large paddles on a patient's chest, delivering a shock that brings the patient back from the dead. This act is known as defibrillation, and how it is portrayed in movies is only partially accurate. Cardiac defibrillators are machines that shock a person's heart back into a proper rhythm. Jean-Louis Prevost and Frederic Batelli invented the device in 1899, although it was only used on dogs at this time to show potential for human usage. Advancements were made that eventually made it suitable for medical usage. However, unlike what is shown on television, the device cannot shock a non-beating heart back into beating. Instead, it is meant to shock a heart having arrhythmias back into a proper rhythm. This is why defibrillators are often used in CPR only after a heartbeat is found. Despite being unable to resuscitate a patient without a heartbeat, cardiac defibrillators have saved many lives and will likely continue to save many more.

66. Soap

Soap is a product created for the purpose of cleaning objects and people. Soaps come from fatty acids, with soapmakers combining an alkyl with metal to produce a specific type of product. Early records indicate that the first instance of soapmaking may have occurred in 2800 BC, in Babylon, by combining oils and wood ash. Later cultures used animal fats alongside various oils and ashes. Soap was initially used to clean fabric. The Gauls were among the first people to openly record using the product to clean the body, although it is likely other cultures used it similarly and did not keep a record of it. Over time, animal fat became less popular as an ingredient due to the unpleasant smell it caused some soaps to have. While various oils were used to replace it, olive oil was by far the most popular due to its neutral scent. Specially scented soap would not gain significant popularity until after the industrial revolution when mass production had been established. Overall, soap aids us in keeping ourselves and our world clean.

67. Moving assembly line

Before the moving assembly line was invented, workers spent a significant amount of time moving to find products and tools. The moving assembly line took conveyor belts that were commonly used in food production and introduced them to the manufacturing industry. Workers were given a single role, and a conveyor belt brought the materials to work, reducing the energy and time required to make products. The inventor of this method was Henry Ford. Ford used this method to make assembling automobiles a simple, streamlined process. The process officially began in 1913 at the Highland Park assembly plant. This led to the Model T being built in an hour and a half. While workers found the process tedious, Ford overcame this concern by doubling his employees' pay. Soon, workers were flocking to work for him, and other manufacturers were implementing the same method. Thus, the creation of the moving assembly line changed not only the manufacturing process of automobiles but the expected pay of those building them.

68. Telescope

Humanity has always been interested in the sky above us, and specifically, humans have been especially interested in the stars and planets in our night sky. Galileo built one of the first telescopes in 1609, using information from a patent by Hans Lipperhey in 1608. These telescopes used refraction to enhance images of the night sky. Later, in 1668, Isaac Newton built a telescope that used reflection instead of refraction. Advancements continued to be made, and the clarity of the device continued to improve. Telescopes led to an increased understanding of outer space, the planets, and the stars. They aided us in recognizing the movement patterns of our solar system, clearly seeing the surfaces of other planets, and discovering new planets. Modern telescopes, such as the Hubble Telescope, are so powerful that they can even allow us to view other galaxies that are millions of miles away.

69. Radio

The radio is a communication device that works primarily via radio waves. The waves are sent out via a transmitter and then are picked up by a radio receiver. The inventor of the technology has been a controversial topic. Some argue that Nikola Tesla invented the radio, while others attribute it to Guglielmo Marconi. The first broadcast to a large audience was done by Charles Herrold in 1910. Originally, broadcasts were entirely informational. Radio broadcasting for the purpose of entertainment was not considered until 1920, when segments of live performances were aired. The device was extremely popular by the 1930s, with most households owning a radio and many colleges offering radio broadcasting courses. Today, the radio is used to transmit news, entertainment, education, and music. While the popularity of traditional radios is lessening, broadcasters have managed to fight this by adding their broadcasts to smartphone apps. The future of radio is uncertain, but ultimately, it played an important role in historical communication.

70. Cloud storage systems

From tangible devices to nebulous virtual realms, the story of data storage is a tale of relentless innovation. In the past, while tools like floppy disks, CD ROMs, and USB drives marked significant leaps, they had an inherent limitation: physicality. Lose the device, and you were often out of luck with your data. Cloud storage emerged as the antidote to this predicament, offering a platform where data wasn't tied to a specific device but saved in virtual spaces managed by tech companies. Though the idea's seed was planted in the 1960s with J.C.R. Licklider's ARPANET, the mainstream embrace of cloud storage awaited Amazon Web Services and its 2006 launch of Amazon S3, heralding a new chapter in how we store and access our digital treasures.

71. Dialysis machine

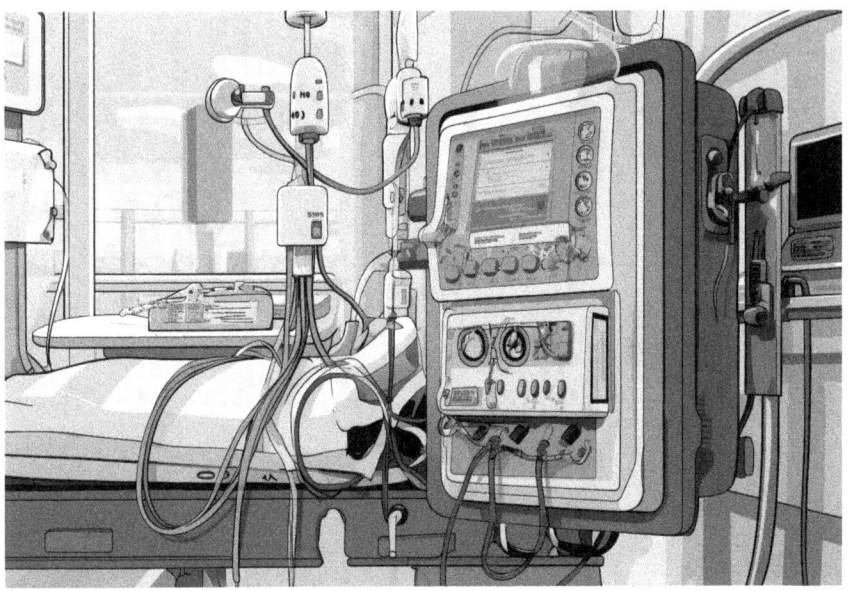

Kidney failure is a terrifying reality for a large number of people. However, the concept was even scarier before the invention of the dialysis machine. The kidneys work to remove toxins from the human body. Kidney failure results in a build-up of unwanted toxins that can poison us. Dialysis is a process that uses a machine to filter out these toxins when the kidneys cannot do so themselves. The dialysis machine was first successfully used in 1943 and has been in use since then. Typically, dialysis is a temporary measure, either to help individuals with kidney injuries heal or to support them until they receive a transplant. However, some people who cannot get transplants remain on dialysis for the rest of their lives. For these individuals, dialysis can add years to their lifespan and improve their quality of life. The dialysis machine has saved countless lives since its invention, and improvements in the science of dialysis are still being pursued.

72. Public trash disposal

In ancient times, human waste disposal was not a major concern as most waste produced by early humans consisted of biodegradable materials. A small number of humans tended to live together in groups, especially in comparison to modern populations. This meant that waste could safely be left to biodegrade. However, with changes in the type of waste produced and a growing population, humanity could only maintain this process for a while. Around the 1700s, waste began to build up in cities, leading to sanitation and health concerns. However, it was only in the cholera outbreaks of the 1800s that this issue was taken seriously. In 1846, the United Kingdom passed the Nuisance Removal and Disease Prevention Act, which began the quest for waste management. In 1875, the Public Health Act was passed, creating and enforcing the use of trash cans. These practices eventually spread to the rest of the Western world, and soon most municipal governments had some form of waste disposal.

73. Toothpaste

We often take this invention for granted, not realizing that the minty paste once did not exist. Toothpaste is a product used to clean the teeth and protect it from further damage. A variety of toothpaste now exists in different flavors and for various purposes. Early toothpaste was made from similar ingredients to soap mixed with abrasives to help scrape gunk off teeth. In the 1800s, toothpowder was invented using ground-up chalk and charcoal. Many tooth powders did more harm than good and removed the teeth' enamel. Arm and Hammer had a helpful version of this tooth powder made primarily from baking soda. Early toothpaste recipes included odd ingredients such as burnt bread. Eventually, the Colgate company released the first toothpaste similar to the one we know today. In 1900, toothpaste with the main ingredients of hydrogen peroxide and baking soda was created. These ingredients are still often used today in toothpaste production as they help whiten teeth and kill germs that cause cavities.

74. Public libraries

The modern world relies on using the Internet to store and share information. While humans still use books for this, they are less necessary for this purpose than before the invention of the World Wide Web. However, even when books were an essential source of knowledge, they were not always easily available. Public libraries were an attempt to allow the general public to access this information before the time of the Internet. These libraries were often publicly funded, and access was granted either for free or at a very low cost. The first public libraries are of Sumerian origin. These libraries did not even have books but instead had clay tablets available to read, mainly consisting of data collection and historical records. Libraries such as these continued to be built in various cities; sometimes, they were funded by the government, but other times the church funded them. Libraries became increasingly accessible during the 1700s, and today, even small towns often have a local library. The creation of these services has led to a more intelligent, better-informed society.

75. Fertilizer

When attempting to grow plants, one must ensure they are using nutrient-rich soil. If the location's soil is not naturally nutrient-rich, it is often best to treat the soil with fertilizer. Fertilizer has been used since ancient times, and records indicate it was popular in ancient Egypt and Babylon. While early fertilizer was not formulated like today's fertilizer, it was still effective as it primarily uses specific nutrients such as nitrogen or manure, which is still used in modern fertilizer due to its effectiveness. Over time, additional additives were found to also be effective in creating fertilizer. This included bonemeal, sulfuric acid, and various phosphates. The creation and production of fertilizer benefited many gardeners and individuals growing home gardens. However, the individuals who benefited most were those who worked in agriculture. Agricultural workers relied on nutrient-rich soil to produce goods. Failure to produce these goods resulted in lost wages and potentially lost employment. The mass production of fertilizer allowed the agriculture industry to fight back against soil that had lost its nutrients and ensured successful harvests regardless of location.

76. EMDR Therapy

EMDR therapy, also known as eye movement desensitization and reprocessing therapy, is used to treat post-traumatic stress disorder symptoms. This method works as follows: the patient is told to focus on specific traumatic memories while moving their eyes from side to side in a specific, repetitive manner. This technique was invented by Francine Shapiro in the 1980s. While a lot of controversy surrounds the practice as nobody quite understands exactly what role eye movements play in helping patients overcome traumatic memories, evidence has shown it to be an effective treatment for post-traumatic stress disorder and related issues. Health organizations and governments worldwide now recommend this treatment to those who suffer from traumatic memories. Many individuals who have received this treatment claim that it has helped them drastically when other treatments were ineffective. Thus, EMDR therapy has allowed for an effective treatment that otherwise may not be possible.

77. Pasteurization

Pasteurization is a process where products are treated with low amounts of heat to kill bacteria. This not only makes products safer but also extends their shelf life. The process was invented by and named after Louis Pasteur in the 1860s, and its original purpose was the treatment of wine. Today, the most commonly known pasteurized product on the market is pasteurized milk. Other products that undergo the process of pasteurization before sale are alcohol, canned foods, dairy products, vinegars, and syrups. Specific pathogens that are removed using this method include Staphylococcus aureus and Salmonella. Some people complain that pasteurized products lose their quality and taste different. However, most people consider it a small price to pay to avoid food-borne illnesses. New methods of pasteurization continue to be invented, allowing for even more pathogens to be removed from the food.

78. Barometer

While many individuals have heard of the thermometer, fewer individuals are aware of its sister device, the barometer. A barometer is a tool that is used to measure air pressure. While this doesn't sound like something that would matter to most people, barometers are excellent indicators of weather change. Before the weather changes, subtle modifications in the air pressure take place. With barometers, it is possible to predict weather changes long before they actually happen. Evangelista Torriceli invented the first barometer in the 1600s. However, the device was not used for weather forecasting until the 1800s. Meteorologists pair barometer readings with wind speed and direction readings to predict short-term weather patterns. Modern meteorologists exchange barometer readings amongst themselves to create an air pressure map. This makes it possible to give longer-term predictions regarding weather patterns. Thus, the creation of the barometer has helped people prepare for and avoid potential weather disasters and has made predicting the weather much easier.

79. Microscope

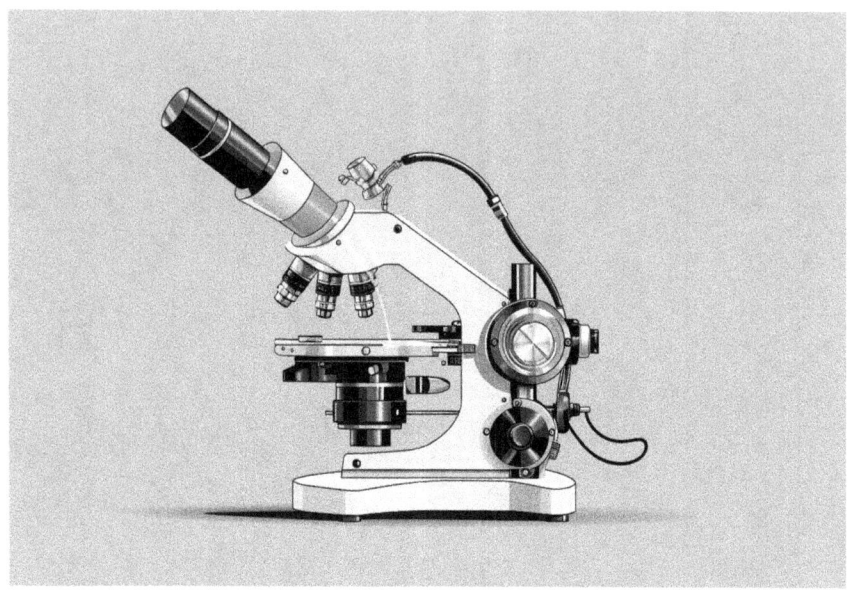

The world around us is composed of organisms that are so small that we cannot naturally see them just by looking at them. Instead, these organisms must be viewed through a special tool referred to as a microscope. Early microscopes were invented in the 1600s and used compound lenses to view microorganisms. These devices did not catch on until around 1650, when scientists began using them to study biology and medicine. Microscopes during this time were referred to as light microscopes due to their usage of condenser lenses to focus light on specific areas of a specimen. This led to the eventual discovery of spermatozoa and blood cells, prompting additional advancements to be made to the device. Eventually, the mighty electron microscope was created, which allowed for higher resolutions and visualization of even smaller organisms. Today, microscopes are still used regularly in the medical field and in various types of research. Without this invention, we would still be completely unaware of the microscopic world.

80. Compression socks

Sometimes, excessive standing or walking can cause blood to pool in the lower legs. This can lead to a range of issues, the most prevalent being leg pain. For individuals who already have cardiovascular problems, the consequences of blood pooling can be more severe. Thrombosis and edema can be an unfortunate consequence of blood pooling in the lower legs. Luckily, compression socks and stockings are inventions designed to counteract the accumulation of blood in the lower extremities. These garments produce pressure on the feet, ankles, and legs, preventing blood from pooling and increasing the effectiveness of arteries and veins. Tailored medical garments are crafted for individuals dealing with cardiovascular disorders. These specialized compression stockings are significantly more robust than their off-the-shelf counterparts. Over-the-counter compression socks, on the other hand, cater to athletes and those with occupations involving extended standing. While they may not address cardiovascular conditions, they can aid in averting unwarranted discomfort in the lower legs.

Did You Know?

The Golden Ratio, often represented by the Greek letter φ (Phi), is a mathematical constant approximately equal to 1.61803398875. This number has intrigued mathematicians, artists, architects, and naturalists alike for its surprising and recurrent appearance in various fields.

Its allure lies in its perceived natural balance and beauty. Here's how the Golden Ratio has echoed through history and disciplines:

- Art: Renowned artists, such as Leonardo da Vinci, are believed to have used the Golden Ratio in their masterpieces like the Mona Lisa, asserting an aesthetic appeal that is innately pleasing to the human eye.

- Architecture: The Parthenon in Athens, a temple dedicated to the goddess Athena, showcases proportions that embody the Golden Ratio, highlighting its timeless architectural beauty.

- Nature: The spiral arrangement of leaves and flowers in plants, the pattern of seeds in a sunflower, and the spiral in galaxies like the Milky Way all display this unique proportion. Even the breeding patterns of rabbits, as explored by Leonardo of Pisa in the Fibonacci sequence, approach the Golden Ratio.

- Human Body: The proportion of our finger bones, the layout of our facial features, and other body proportions often reflect the Golden Ratio. Some suggest this proportion is a universal standard of beauty.

The Golden Ratio stands as a testament to the interconnectedness of mathematics with the natural and human-made world, acting as an underlying thread that weaves its way through the tapestry of time and culture.

81. Atomic bomb

The atomic bomb is an invention that has been particularly useful and harmful to humanity. The first nuclear bomb that was successfully deployed was built by the United States government. This bomb was dropped on the Japanese city of Hiroshima during World War II on August 6th, 1945. An additional bomb was dropped on Nagasaki three days later, on August 9th. These bombs cause mass destruction of buildings, thousands of deaths due to the immediate effects of the blast, and thousands more deaths due to radiation poisoning. They were dropped in retaliation for an attack on Pearl Harbor, a naval base located in Hawaii. Since these attacks, the atomic bomb has not been used in warfare. Several countries have developed atomic bombs and have deployed them in test experiments. However, employing these weapons in combat would pose an existential threat to humanity, as the potential for retaliation could result in an escalation of nuclear strikes. The radiation aftermath from multiple detonations would extend across continents. Consequently, many diplomatic discussions among countries revolve around strategies to avert the specter of nuclear conflict.

82. Text messaging

After the creation of the cell phone, it was more accessible than ever to call people no matter where you were. However, many people felt that making phone calls was not truly convenient, even if they could do it on the go. Text messaging was invented to communicate without having to call people. SMS (or Short Message Service) messages were the first text messages to be sent via mobile phone. This messaging technique was officially open for public use in 1994. Early text messaging systems required users to belong to the same phone network; it wasn't until a few years later that cross-network connectivity was possible. Despite these advancements, text messaging on early phones took a lot of work as there was a limited keypad requiring multiple clicks to choose a letter. By the mid-2000s, unlimited texting was a common feature in most phone plans, with phones having an alphanumeric keypad similar to what one would find on a laptop computer. During this period, texting gained popularity, and nowadays, most people use this service on their phones every day.

83. Heart-lung machine

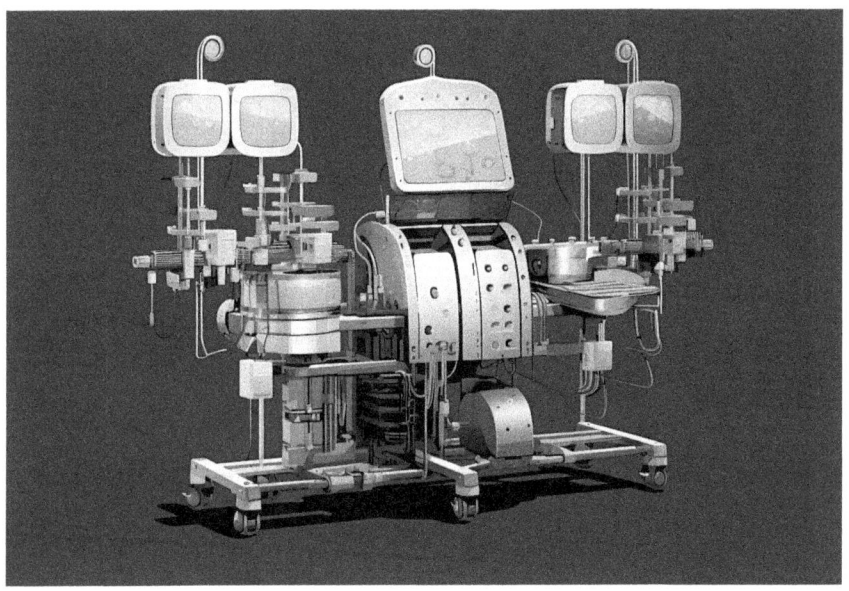

The heart-lung machine, officially known as the cardiopulmonary bypass machine, is a machine that temporarily takes over the functions of breathing and blood circulation for the human body. This device is most often used in cardiac surgery as the effects of anesthetics and paralytics sometimes interfere with a patient's ability to breathe and regulate their heart rate on their own, especially if the heart is actively being worked on. Although blueprints for the machine were created in the early 1900s, it was not until 1951 that it was successfully used on a human patient. However, the patient later died due to unrelated complications from a heart defect. Today, this apparatus is used routinely in cardiac surgeries and is controlled by a perfusionist. Although there are risks associated with its usage, they are rare. However, the longer a patient is on the machine, the more of a chance of complications that patient has. That is why it's only used during surgery, and other devices are employed if longer-term care is needed.

84. Non-steroidal anti-inflammatory drugs

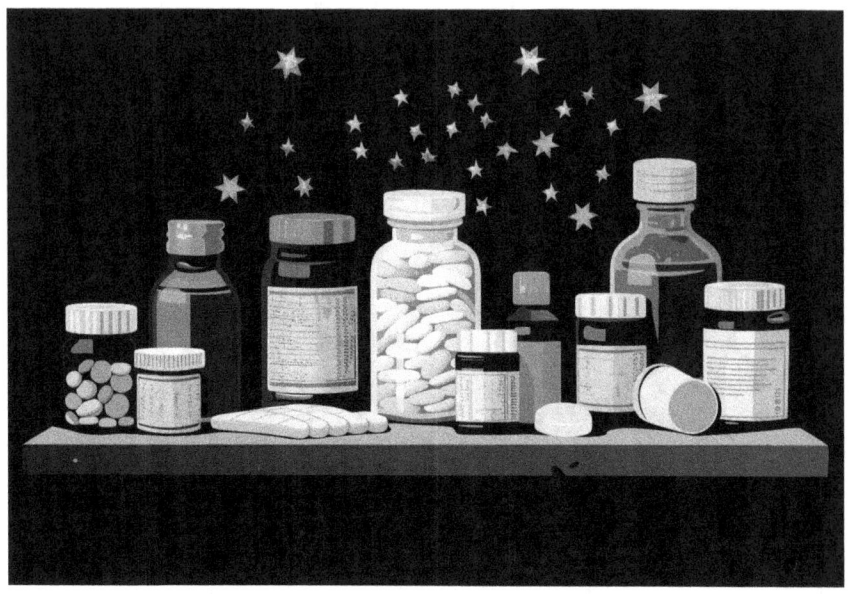

The most common treatment for inflammation in the body is the usage of steroids. However, their utilization comes with several side effects, and long-term use can cause complications such as insulin resistance and lowered immune system development. The development of non-steroidal anti-inflammatory drugs, or NSAIDs, allows for treating inflammation with a lessened risk of severe side effects. These drugs include aspirin, naproxen, and ibuprofen. The first NSAID to be developed was aspirin, created in 1897 by Felix Hoffman. Later NSAIDs were not developed until the 1950s. These drugs are used to treat various illnesses and conditions, including chronic pain and inflammation, and help prevent blood clotting. Often, the only alternatives to NSAIDs are steroids, which can cause dangerous side effects, and opioids, which can lead to addiction. Hence, NSAIDs have emerged as a widely used remedy for pain arising from inflammation or discomfort that doesn't necessitate the potential risks associated with steroids or opioids.

85. Television

Television is a common fixture in a majority of households across the world, so it is difficult to imagine a time when this device did not exist. Yet, until the 1920s, this appliance was not yet even a thought inside somebody's head. Around that time, John Logie Baird invented the first television, changing how humans communicate and entertain themselves forever. The first thirty years or so after the invention of the television consisted of public displays to gain attention, the creation of television broadcasts, and troubleshooting malfunctions as they arose. Finally, in the 1950s, they began purchasing televisions for home usage and started using them as their primary media source. This model facilitated news delivery, marking the onset of radio news and newspaper usage decline. Advancements were made, leading to the creation of the color television and increased screen size. Soon, older bulky models were replaced by flat-screen models. Today, many televisions have additional functionalities, such as Internet connectivity. Their capabilities continue to change with new technological advances.

86. Petrol

Petrol, or gasoline, is a liquid created from distilling petroleum. It is used as a fuel source in combustion engines and is the most common energy source for motor vehicles. Edwin Drake first discovered gasoline by accident when refining crude oil into kerosene. Gasoline is a byproduct of this process. At the time, this product was not used, so gasoline was often burned off in refineries. Eventually, however, Nicolaus Otto created a combustion engine that could run off the substance. This replaced previous engines that relied on highly volatile liquids. Gasoline quickly began to replace other materials as well, such as coal. In World War I, gasoline emerged as a critical aviation fuel, increasing demand to support the war endeavors. Today, petrol continues to be the primary fuel source used in automobiles. Additional uses include fuel for small watercrafts and aircraft, and as an ingredient in various equipment used in construction. Thus, gasoline drastically changed the transportation industry.

87. Beta-blockers

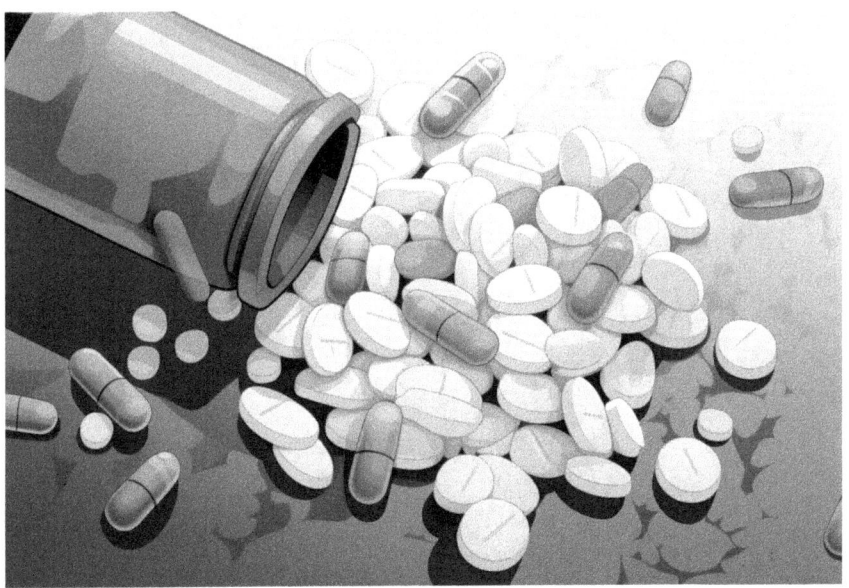

Beta-blockers are drugs known as competitive antagonists. By blocking the ability of the body to use adrenaline and noradrenaline, beta-blockers can prevent a variety of concerning conditions, such as heart arrhythmia (when the heart beats at the wrong speed or pace). This class of drug was invented by James Black in 1964 when he created propranolol and pronethalol. Eventually, more drugs of this type were developed, such as nadolol and atenolol. These drugs changed how many heart conditions are treated and led to more effective management of cardiovascular diseases. The following conditions are now commonly managed via beta-blockers: hypertension, angina, heart attack prevention, arrhythmias, heart failure, migraine, certain types of tremors, and certain anxiety disorders. Without beta-blockers, riskier and less efficient treatment methods would primarily be employed for managing many of these disorders. Thus, beta-blockers have made treatment for these illnesses safer and more effective.

88. VHS

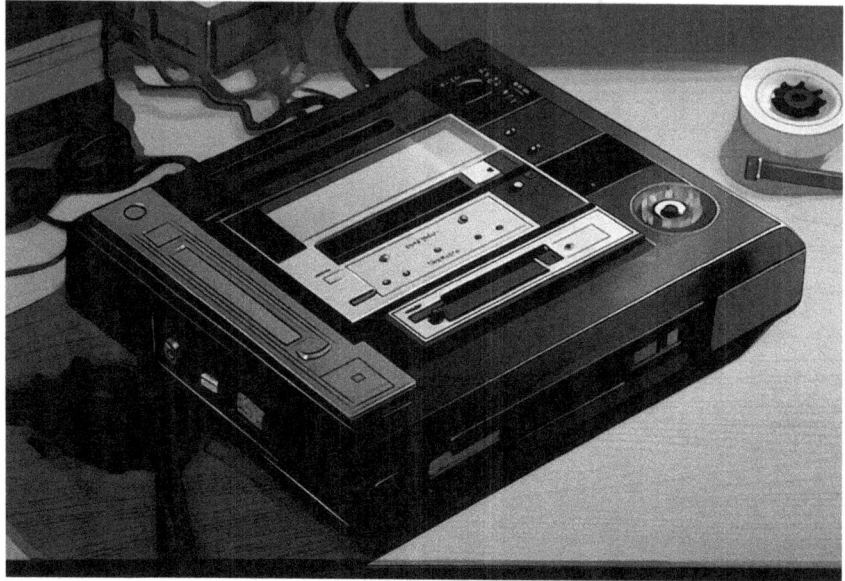

The VHS, also known as the Video Home System, was a cassette tape that allowed individuals to play movies and TV shows on television using a particular VHS player. The device was invented in the 1950s but was only used in professional environments due to the expense of production. It was in the 1970s that home use of the product became affordable. These devices were the first to allow people to watch their favorite movies and shows at home without relying on cable or broadcasting over satellite dishes. It became possible to collect one's favorite shows to watch repeatedly. This changed the way that people watched movies and television. The VHS player fell out of favor due to the creation of more convenient products such as the DVD player. While today the usage of VHS players is not common, people still retain the repetitive viewing habits created by this product.

89. Public transportation

Public transportation is commonly associated with buses and subways available for general use. Although these are prevalent forms today, public transportation has ancient roots. In earlier times, people traveled primarily on foot or by riding animals like donkeys and horses. Travel over water, however, was generally only possible if one owned their own boat. As a result, some ancient cities began to provide ferries for public use. Eventually, the need to travel farther distances over land became commonplace, leading to the invention of public stage coaches, which were carts pulled by horses that citizens could ride in to travel long distances. Soon, horse-drawn boats and horse-drawn railways also became common. Finally, with advances in motorized automobiles, buses, and trams became large cities' primary public transportation source. Today, while many own vehicles, public transportation is still often used due to high fuel prices and the lesser environmental impact of sharing rides versus driving one's own car. In addition, public transportation has made traveling much more affordable for those who do not have cars of their own.

90. Theory of evolution

The theory of evolution as we know it was created when Charles Darwin wrote his famous book, *On the Origins of Species*. Before this theory was discovered, people assumed that there was no link between species. Occasionally, when connections between two species were obvious (such as with wolves and coyotes), people would assume a relation but never think the species stemmed from a similar source. When Darwin proposed his theories, many individuals were upset as they directly opposed religious literalism and the story of creation in the *Bible*. However, over time the theory has been accepted as accurate, at least on a microscale, as changes to species have since been recorded. The theory states that new species form when existing species adapt to their environment via natural selection. Certain traits are removed, and others are introduced, leading to the creation of new species. This theory has aided us in connecting various species of the animal kingdom, which has also allowed us to learn more about now-extinct animals. While some individuals still consider the theory controversial, it is accepted as fact and taught in most schools.

91. Carbon dating

Carbon dating, also known as radiocarbon dating, is a method of determining the age of an object invented by Willard Libby in 1947. The process only works on organic materials or things that were once living. This is because the method relies on radiocarbon, an isotope of the carbon found in living creatures that are radioactive. Radioactive carbon is created in the atmosphere and absorbed by plants. Animals eat these plants, and other animals eat the plant-eating animals spreading the radioactive carbon throughout the food chain. Once an organism dies, they ingest no more radioactive carbon. The isotope begins to decay upon death and has a half-life of almost 6,000 years. Scientists can measure the amount of this radioactive isotope in an object to determine how long ago it stopped ingesting carbon. The process only works on creatures that were alive less than 50,000 years ago, but this is more than enough to give us information that we did not previously have about the species that existed before us.

92. Hindu Arabic numeral system

The Hindu Arabic numeral system was invented sometime between 1 and 3000 AD. This was the first system to use ten digits placed in different sequences to represent various numbers. The addition of a decimal also could lead to portions of a whole being represented via the symbols. Multiple variations of the system exist, with the globally recognized version being the Western Arabic numeral system. The numbers zero through nine make up the system and are combined to produce multi-digit numbers. The Eastern Arabic numeral system is the other system that is still in use, although its usage is limited to countries in the Middle East. It is incredibly similar as it has ten different symbols representing the numbers through nine, which can be arranged similarly to the Western Arabic numeral system.

93. Smartphone

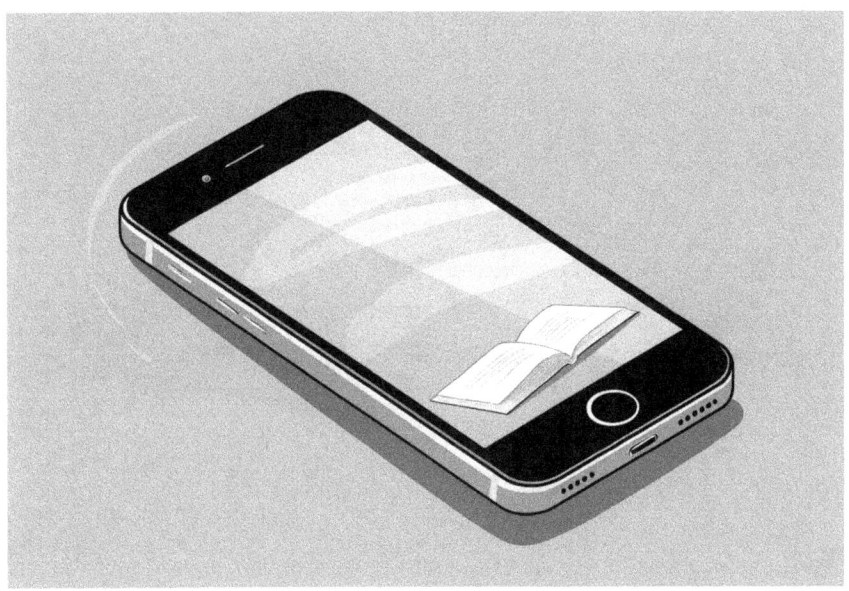

The smartphone, far more than a mere cellular device, embodies the evolution of digital communication and computing. Emerging from the nascent ideas of the 1990s, early iterations were an ambitious blend of the cell phone and the personal digital assistant (PDA). Yet, these trailblazers faced skepticism, burdened by their unwieldy size and fleeting battery life. As the millennium turned, technological advancements, particularly in the late 2000s and early 2010s, transformed the smartphone's narrative. Suddenly, these devices weren't just for calling and texting. They blossomed into compact powerhouses, mirroring the capabilities of full-fledged computers. With a myriad of applications at one's fingertips, users could seamlessly transition from gaming to media streaming, social networking to browsing, and even document editing. In essence, the modern smartphone is a testament to our perennial aspiration — to encapsulate the vast world of computing and the infinite web of connectivity within the confines of our pockets.

94. DVD

Many individuals born before the early 2000s remember a time when VHS tapes were the primary way to watch movies and television shows that we're not currently playing on cable or satellite dishes. These people may recall the tedious task of rewinding these VHS tapes and the frustration of having a tape become damaged and unable to play. The DVD, also known as the Digital Versatile Disc, was invented to combat the limitations of the VHS tape. While the product was created in 1996, it did not reach mainstream success until around 2000. Soon after, DVD player sales began to overtake VHS players, and several gaming consoles were outfitted with DVD-playing capabilities. DVDs had several features that VHS tapes could not have, such as the ability to select specific movie scenes for playback directly, the inclusion of supplementary special features like interactive games, and the provision of audio options in various languages. As streaming services have become more prevalent in recent years, DVDs are still the primary way that people store movies and television shows they want to keep a physical copy of to watch repeatedly.

95. Refrigerator

Have you ever heard an elderly person refer to a refrigerator as an ice box? There is a reason that some older individuals use that term. In the 1930s, refrigerators were found in most households. Instead, wooden boxes kept cool via ice were used to store cold food items. Despite this, the technology for refrigerators was invented in 1755 by William Cullen. Unfortunately, early models were often dangerous and easily broken. However, by 1860, some models were commercially available, keeping items in meat packing plants and breweries from spoiling. These models sometimes leak ammonia and sulfur dioxide, making them too dangerous and costly for residential usage. Only when a much safer compound, freon, replaced these chemicals did home usage begin to become popular. Finally, people could safely and efficiently store cold food items without handling large blocks of melting ice.

96. Dentures

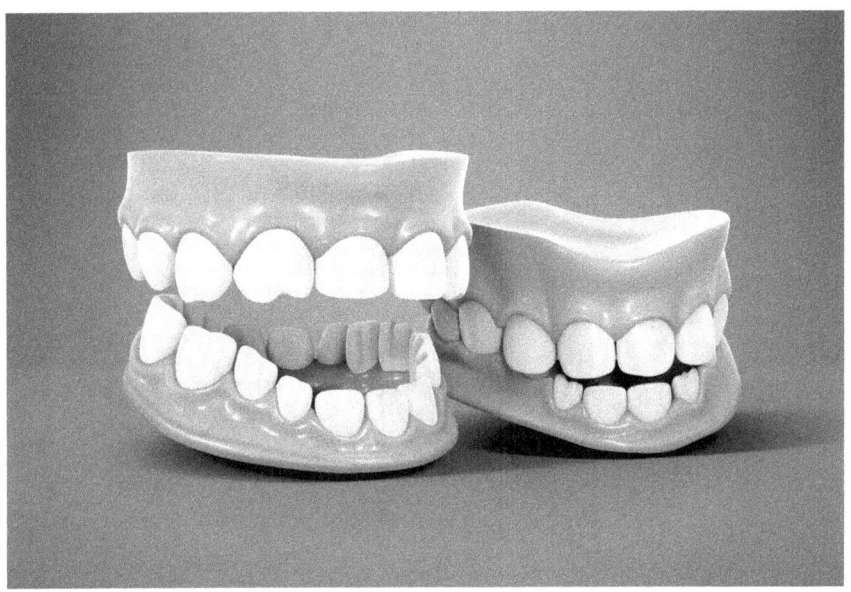

While dentures don't necessarily seem like anything special today, their invention changed many individuals' lives. Early sets of dentures were made from actual teeth taken from human beings or animals. This was the process used during ancient times and continued to be used until more modern product variations were invented. In the 16th century, the Japanese began using wood to create their dentures. Finally, in 1770, the first set of porcelain dentures was made by Alexis Duchateau. While everybody knows that one of the main benefits of dentures is that the individual can chew and eat as normal, people need to realize that there are other ways that dentures benefit those who wear them. Without dentures, the bones and tissues of the mouth and jaw shift and change uncontrollably. This can lead to pain and disfigurement as time goes on. The invention of dentures didn't just allow people to eat comfortably, but it also prevented excess pain and potential undesirable facial changes. Thus, dentures have drastically changed the lives of those who do not have teeth.

97. Prozac

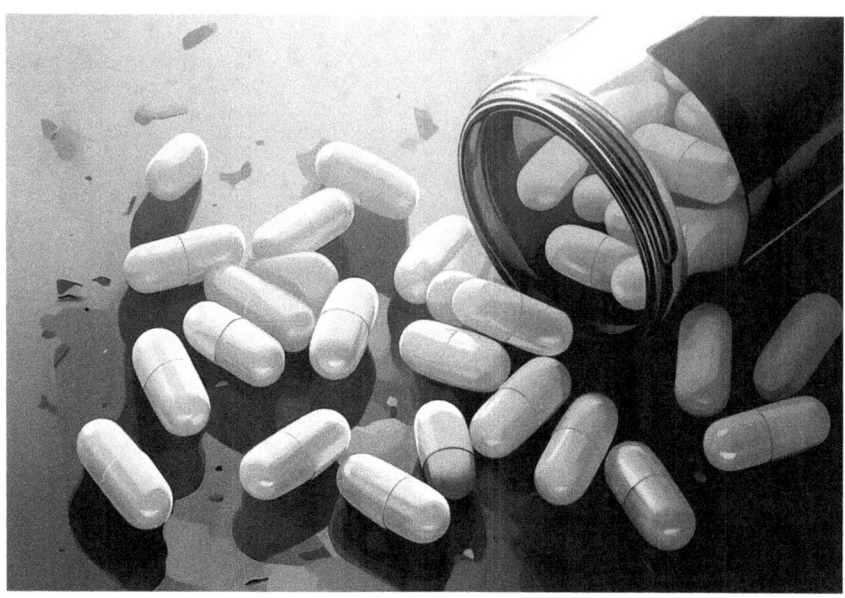

Prozac, also known as fluoxetine, belongs to a class of medications referred to as serotonin reuptake inhibitors. This medication helps prevent the symptoms of certain mental disorders such as obsessive-compulsive disorder, major depressive disorder, and generalized anxiety disorder. This is done via the medication blocking the body's ability to reabsorb and eliminate excess serotonin, a chemical in the brain responsible for happiness, forcing the brain to use the entire supply. Individuals with the above disorders are believed to produce enough serotonin, but the body disposes of most of it before it can be used. Prozac was discovered in 1974 by David T. Wong. Since then, it has become widely prescribed and has led to the discovery of several similar drugs, such as Zoloft (sertraline), Lexapro (escitalopram), and Celexa (citalopram). The side effects of these drugs are minimal compared to other anti-depressants and anti-anxiety medications. Being the first line of pharmacological treatment for many mental disorders,

Prozac and other SSRIs (selective serotonin reuptake inhibitors) have made treatment easier and safer.

98. Electric motor

An electric motor is a machine that uses electricity to create mechanical energy. The device relies on an electromagnetic field to fuel the product and can be powered by sources such as batteries or electricity on an electrical grid. The engine works by creating force via torque. William Sturgeon invented the first battery-operated electrical motor in 1832. These battery-operated motors were used in various machinery, including handheld tools and kitchen appliances. In addition, they were sometimes used to power printing presses. With the development of new technologies, motors became more durable and quieter and were gradually used in more products. They found applications in automating labor, creating HVAC systems, and various manufacturing jobs. Eventually, electrical engines led to the invention of elevators and escalators. These motors were genuinely innovative in their ability to run on batteries and the electrical grid. They were instrumental in advancing small appliances, many of which could not have been invented otherwise.

99. Dental braces

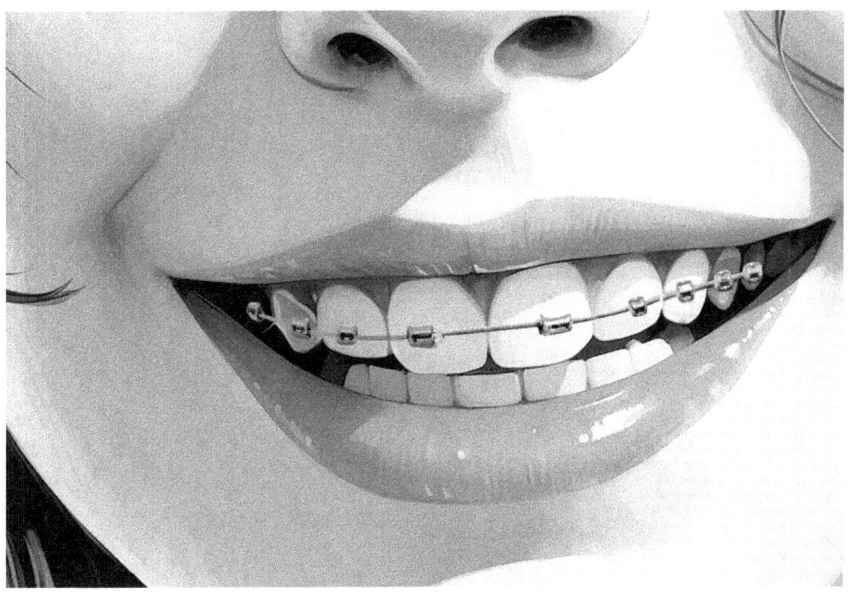

While nobody enjoys getting braces, they play a significant role in oral hygiene and health. Their invention allowed dentists and orthodontists to solve issues that were essentially untreatable in the past. Dental braces or devices are used to move the teeth in a person's mouth. Wires and hooks are used to put pressure on various parts of the mouth and slowly force the mouth, teeth, and jaw to move into a desired position. Christophe-Francois Delabarre invented this process, and it was primarily done with wires. Eventually, additional equipment was added to the process, including rubber bands and hooks. Over time, dental braces became more common and available for use. The increased use of dental braces has reduced dental problems caused by poor oral hygiene, speech impediments, and periodontal disease (also known as gum disease).

100. Air conditioner

For the majority of history, cooling one's house was a matter of using a passive technique. Homes were built so that the architecture would encourage cooling if the house were located in a warm climate. In addition, windows were often left open to promote cooling during the hot summer months. While this was effective in keeping temperatures inside of a house at a safe level, it did not necessarily help keep them at a comfortable level. In 1901, Willis H. Carrier invented the first modern air conditioning unit, changing how we handle the temperature of our homes. Initially, these air conditioning units were used in commercial business and manufacturing. Business owners often wanted to keep their goods in a climate-controlled environment. In 1914, the device finally became available for domestic use. Since then, it has been improved upon several times, with the first time being the invention of the window unit. Over time, every generation of air conditioning models has been enhanced in effectiveness, power, and durability, ensuring human comfort and well-being during hot weather.

Did You Know?

The concept of "multiple discovery" or "simultaneous invention" refers to the phenomenon where multiple scientists or inventors, working independently, come to the same discovery or invention roughly at the same time. This intriguing occurrence highlights the idea that when the right societal, technological, and intellectual foundations are present, it's possible for different individuals to converge on the same innovative thought or solution.

Historically, there have been numerous instances of multiple discoveries. Some famous examples include:

• Atomic Theory: John Dalton in England and Amedeo Avogadro in Italy both contributed significantly to the development of atomic theory in the early 19th century, although they approached the topic from different angles and based on different evidence.

• The Electric Telegraph: Multiple inventors, including Samuel Morse in the United States and Sir William Fothergill Cooke and Charles Wheatstone in Britain, developed variations of the telegraph during the same period in the 1830s.

• Relativity Theory: While Albert Einstein is the most famous name associated with the theory of relativity, Hendrik Lorentz and Henri Poincaré made significant contributions to the same ideas and concepts around the same time in the early 20th century.

These examples, among many others, demonstrate that the broader environment—consisting of prior knowledge, societal needs, and available technologies—can often set the stage for multiple individuals to arrive at the same or similar conclusions or inventions simultaneously.

101. Calculus

Calculus is often a topic that people tend to joke about due to its rigor and difficulty. However, the subject of calculus and its invention has benefited humanity quite a bit. Calculus is the type of math that studies the numbers behind the continuous change. The subject was actually invented by two people at the same time, with both being completely unaware of the work of the other. Sir Isaac Newton and Gottfried Wilhelm Leibniz both invented calculus and published the concept at the same time in the 17th century. The invention of the study greatly impacted engineering, with structural, civil, mechanical, and electrical engineering all benefitting. In addition, calculus has improved the medical field, allowing doctors to properly assess a patient's condition using the data found in tests. Calculus is also used in research analysis, meteorology, music, and business. All these fields require one to track changes, leading to the implementation of calculus. Thus, humanity would be years behind in all subjects had calculus not been invented.

References

"About Calculus." American Mathematical Society. Accessed August 29, 2023. https://www.ams.org/publications/journals/notices/201702/rnoti-p209.pdf.

"About the Computer Mouse." The Doug Engelbart Institute. Accessed July 31, 2023. http://www.dougengelbart.org/about/mouse.html.

"A Brief History of Wi-Fi." The Economist. Last modified August 27, 2022. https://www.economist.com/.

"A History of Vaccines." The History of Vaccines, The College of Physicians of Philadelphia. Last updated March 14, 2023. https://www.historyofvaccines.org/.

Carson, Mary Kay. Alexander Graham Bell: National Geographic Kids. National Geographic Children's Books, 2013. (For Telephone)

Diamond, Jared. 1997. Guns, Germs, and Steel: The Fates of Human Societies. New York: W. W. Norton & Company.

"Elon Musk and the Future of Electric Cars." Tesla Motors Official Blog. Accessed August 5, 2023. https://www.tesla.com/blog.

"Global Positioning System History." NASA. Last modified June 22, 2021. https://www.nasa.gov/directorates/heo/scan/communications/policy/GPS_History.html.

Freeberg, Ernest. The Age of Edison: Electric Light and the Invention of Modern America. Penguin Books, 2014.

Flink, James J. The Automobile Age. MIT Press, 1990.

Gibbs-Smith, Charles. The Wright Brothers: A Brief Account of Their Work, 1899-1911. London: HMSO, 1984.

Hertzfeld, Andy. 2005. Revolution in The Valley: The Insanely Great Story of How the Mac Was Made. Sebastopol, CA: O'Reilly Media.

"How Edison Changed the World." The Thomas Edison Papers, Rutgers University. Last updated December 2, 2021. https://edison.rutgers.edu/.

"The History of the Internet." Internet Society. Last modified January 5, 2022. https://www.internetsociety.org/internet/history-internet/.

"The History of the Wheel." Exploratorium. Last modified January 3, 2022. https://www.exploratorium.edu/wheel/.

"The History of Vaccines and Immunization: Familiar Patterns, New Challenges." The History of Vaccines, The College of Physicians of Philadelphia. Last updated November 10, 2021. https://www.historyofvaccines.org/content/articles/history-vaccines-and-immunization-familiar-patterns-new-challenges.

"Innovation Timeline: Technology Milestones." IEEE Spectrum. Last modified June 16, 2018. https://spectrum.ieee.org/static/interactive-timeline-milestones.

"Introduction to DNA Fingerprinting." Genetics Home Reference, U.S. National Library of Medicine. Last modified May 17, 2022. https://ghr.nlm.nih.gov/primer/testing/genetictesting.

"Introduction to Steam Engines." Smithsonian National Museum of American History. Accessed August 30, 2023. https://americanhistory.si.edu/.

"Inventions That Changed the World." Smithsonian Magazine. Accessed August 1, 2023. https://www.smithsonianmag.com/innovation/inventions-that-changed-the-world/.

Isaacson, Walter. 2014. The Innovators: How a Group of Hackers, Geniuses, and Geeks Created the Digital Revolution. New York: Simon & Schuster.

Johnson, Steven. 2010. Where Good Ideas Come From: The Natural History of Innovation. New York: Riverhead Books.

Johnson, Steven. 2014. How We Got to Now: Six Innovations That Made the Modern World. New York: Riverhead Books.

Johnston, David, and Tom Jenkins. 2017. Ingenious: How Canadian Innovators Made the World Smarter, Smaller, Kinder, Safer, Healthier, Wealthier, and Happier. Toronto: Signal.

Kuhn, Thomas S. The Structure of Scientific Revolutions. 4th ed. University of Chicago Press, 2012.

Lewis, Tom. 1991. Empire of the Air: The Men Who Made Radio. New York: HarperCollins.

"Lightbulb: Edison vs. Swan." Edison Tech Center. Accessed August 30, 2023. http://www.edisontechcenter.org/.

"The Life of Johannes Gutenberg." Gutenberg Museum. Accessed August 29, 2023. https://www.gutenberg-museum.de/en.

McCullough, David. 2015. The Wright Brothers. New York: Simon & Schuster.

Owens, David. The Espresso Quest: In Search of the Perfect Coffee. Transworld Publishers, 1997.

Rosen, William. 2010. The Most Powerful Idea in the World: A Story of Steam, Industry, and Invention. New York: Random House.

Schwartz, Evan I. The Last Lone Inventor: A Tale of Genius, Deceit, and the Birth of Television. HarperCollins, 2002.

"Top 50 Inventions." TIME Magazine. Last modified October 25, 2010. http://content.time.com/time/specials/packages/completelist/0,29569,2026495,00.html.

Turing, Alan. On Computable Numbers, with an Application to the Entscheidungsproblem. London Mathematical Society, 1936.

"The Evolution of Medical Technology: A Historical Overview." MedTech Impact. Last modified May 7, 2019. https://www.medtechimpact.com/the-evolution-of-medical-technology-a-historical-overview/.

"The History of the Telephone." AT&T Archives. Last modified November 7, 2020. https://about.att.com/innovationblog/history_of_telephone.

"The Wright Brothers & The Invention of the Aerial Age." National Air and Space Museum. Accessed July 29, 2023. https://airandspace.si.edu/exhibitions/wright-brothers/online/.

Usher, Abbott Payson. A History of Mechanical Inventions. Revised ed. Dover Publications, 2011.

Rosenblum, Naomi. A World History of Photography. Abbeville Press, 2008.

Standage, Tom. 1998. The Victorian Internet: The Remarkable Story of the Telegraph and the Nineteenth Century's On-line Pioneers. New York: Walker & Company.

Bonus!

Thanks for supporting me and purchasing this book! I'd like to send you some freebies. They include:

- The digital version of *500 World War I & II Facts*

- The digital version of *101 Idioms and Phrases*

- The audiobook for my best seller *1144 Random Facts*

Scan the QR code below, enter your email and I'll send you all the files. Happy reading!

Check out my other books!